T0065458

THE FIRST LADY

*The Process to My Purpose
Believe, Don't Give Up!*

BONITA MITCHELL

WESTBOW
PRESS®
A DIVISION OF THOMAS NELSON
& ZONDERVAN

WestBow Press books may be ordered through booksellers or by contacting:

WestBow Press
A Division of Thomas Nelson & Zondervan
1663 Liberty Drive
Bloomington, IN 47403
www.westbowpress.com
844-714-3454

Cover Clothing Designer: Casual Couture by Clotee, Los Angeles, CA

Scripture taken from the King James Version of the Bible.

ISBN: 978-1-6642-2880-1 (sc)
ISBN: 978-1-6642-2882-5 (hc)
ISBN: 978-1-6642-2881-8 (e)

Library of Congress Control Number: 2021906262

Print information available on the last page.

WestBow Press rev. date: 06/08/2021

CONTENTS

For we wrestle not against flesh and blood, but against principalities, against powers, against the rulers of darkness of this world, against spiritual wickedness in high places.

—Ephesians 6:12 (KJV)

These things I have spoken unto you, that in me ye might have peace. In the world ye shall have tribulation: but be of good cheer; I have overcome the world.

—John 16:33

The thief cometh not, but for to steal, and to kill, and to destroy: I am come that they might have life, and that they might have it more abundantly.

—John 10:10

Let him know, that he which converteth the sinner from the error of his way shall save a soul from death, and shall hide a multitude of sins.

—James 5:20

But Abraham said, Son, remember that thou in thy lifetime receivedst thy good things, and likewise Lazarus evil things: but now he is comforted, and thou art tormented. Then he said, I pray thee therefore, father, that thou wouldest send him to my father's house: For I have five brethren; that he may testify unto them, lest they also come into this place of torment. Abraham saith unto him, They have Moses and the prophets; let them hear them.

—Luke 16:25, 27–29

Let every man abide in the same calling wherein he was called. Art thou called being a servant? Care not for it: but if thou mayest be made free, use it rather. For he that is called in the Lord, being a servant, is the Lord's freeman: likewise also he that is called, being free, is Christ's servant. Ye are bought with a price; be not ye the servants of men. Brethren, let every man, wherein he is called, therein abide with God.

—1 Corinthians 7:20–24

Let your light so shine before men, that they may see your good works, and glorify your Father which is in heaven.

—Matthew 5:16

INTRODUCTION

Submitting to God's Word, Process, and Purpose for My Life

Family is such a powerful word, often referring to father, mother, sister, and brother. It was very difficult for me to understand at a young age the role of being a part of a true family.

The Lord said in Jeremiah 1:5, "Before, I formed thee in the belly I knew thee; and before thou camest forth out of the womb I sanctified thee, and I ordained thee a prophet unto the nations."

If we are to be disciples of God, there is a path that has some rough roads, hills, and valleys.

John 16:33 tells us, "These things I have spoken unto you, that in me ye might have peace. In the world ye shall have tribulation: but be of good cheer; I have overcome the world."

When we hear the word *family* as children, a heartwarming feeling often comes over us. I remember as a child thinking that my family included only blood relatives. We would eat dinner together, go to church, do many fun things, and enjoy each other. No matter what, we would all be together.

My family

Being in church all day on Sundays was the norm for me while growing up. We started at 9 a.m. with Sunday School; 11 a.m. was the Sunday morning church service, 3 p.m. was the afternoon church service, and 6 p.m. was the Baptist Training Union (BTU) service, where we learned about finding scriptures in the Bible. Those days will always be some of the most memorable ones in my life.

Of course, as a little girl, there had to be other reasons to attend church, and there were. Our church was filled with handsome little boys. It made going to church and singing in the choir that much more special. As a child, I was so carefree, without a worry in the world, with my mom and dad, my sisters and brothers all together. We experienced such a unique relationship with the Lord, which I didn't really realize until later in life. I was just a kid! I didn't have any idea that God would use me as an example of just how powerful He really is.

Around age nine, I was baptized, a frightened little girl giving my life to the Lord. I didn't understand that I was signing up to be in the army for Jesus. Yet I would always hear my mother, the deacons of the church, and my grandfather, Henry McAfee, say and sing, "I'm on the battlefield for my Lord." At the time, I did not understand that phrase.

Matthew 10:16 tells us, "I am sending you out like sheep among wolves."

I know the battlefield is where you get shot or you are prepared to shoot someone. I realize now that the battlefield first starts in my mind and, based on my faith and trust in Jesus, determines how I will dwell in the midst of the battle.

I also know that there are two battles: one in the mind and the other a physical battle fought every day with people who have decided not to take on the character of Jesus but instead allow the principalities and powers in high places to control their thinking and their world.

Now that I'm older and have completely given my life over to Jesus, I can truly say I understand what the word *family* really means, in addition to God's intentions for it. We encounter many situations growing up. Choosing to live for God is one that allows us to obtain wisdom and the ability to show compassion, for that's exactly what Jesus did for us. Family is what God created to multiply this world.

God has given me the confidence in whom He is in my life, which allows me to see with my spiritual eye instead of my carnal eye. God says in Ephesians 6:12, "For we wrestle not against flesh and blood, but against principalities, against powers, against the rulers of the darkness of this world, against spiritual wickedness in high places."

"Amazing grace, how sweet the sound that saved a wretch like me. I once was lost but now I'm found, blind but now I see." I am God's amazing grace. I can see clearly now.

As a child, I could see with my physical eye but was too young to see with my spiritual eye. I thank God that now the shackles have fallen from my eyes and the chains are broken.

That little girl who was ruling my forty-year-old body
no longer has power. She has been dethroned.

My every thought, I pray now every day, is taken up and led by The Holy Spirit. My challenges now would be opportunities for me to keep my faith and trust in Jesus and for others to witness just how good and powerful He is as I continue to be guided and directed by Him.

I didn't realize that my mother and father's divorce would be the hardest thing I ever dealt with in my life. My husband's and my separation with the threat of divorce was a close second. I couldn't understand that what appeared to be the end of my life was actually my new beginning and my path to experiencing just how real principalities are. Most importantly, I learned how much more powerful Jesus and the Holy Spirit are in my life when I allow them to take complete control.

These two life-changing situations were the catalyst for my moving to California, where I found myself in the midst of celebrities and situations of which one could only dream. It was a fantasy world where I not only met and worked with Stevie Wonder but also found myself sitting at his baby grand piano singing "All Is Fair in Love," my favorite song since the age of five.

Working with Stevie Wonder was one of the highlights of my life.

As a broken little girl, I dreamed of being in the entertainment industry, looking beautiful, and wearing fabulous gowns. All of this came true through my life of growing pains. I was not only able to see all the beauty and glamour on TV but also the dark and demonic powers in high places in the music and entertainment industry. I traveled all over the country for ten years with Stevie Wonder and met multiple TV personalities.

I truly thought my life was over when my husband and I started to have serious problems, but it too was just the beginning of a great new chapter in my life with Jesus. God allowed me to experience this level of pain as a part of my journey of getting closer to Him and living my purpose.

My life has changed. I'm no longer the same person I used to be. I thank God for allowing the various storms to enter my life in order to save me and to help others.

As you read this book and travel with me through the process of my life, you too will realize that if Jesus is not real and His word is not the center of your life, things will *never* be right, nor will you understand a peace that surpasses all understanding even though everything is breaking loose around you.

When we start to accept, and submit to Jesus as our personal Savior, sometimes things don't get better physically, but they always improve spiritually. The life of my family was one of the situations of sorrow that God used to lead me closer to Him in the end, but growing up in the midst of it all was painful and traumatizing.

Jesus died because He knew we were going to need to be saved from ourselves—our pride and our selfish desires. He sacrificed His life, giving us an example of what happens when we stay focused on the path God has us on.

Even given the humiliation—being beaten, spit upon, and utterly degraded—Jesus never wavered in His faith in His Father or the purpose of His enduring suffering. He didn't allow a spirit of pride and self-pity to overtake His character or the knowledge that He was sacrificed so that we might have eternal life in heaven with Him and our heavenly Father.

Please read this book and allow God's presence to direct you in the same way He guided me. God has allowed principalities and powers in high places to be a catalyst for us to have greater faith in Jesus and the power of His Holy Spirit. As you read about my journey, please view the many trials I experienced as opportunities that led to my awareness of the various spirits that can enter any of us. When we allow the Holy Spirit to dominate our minds, bodies, and souls, nothing can keep us from the sweet presence of Jesus.

I'm now able to help others in a way I never dreamed. I have a level of serenity and security in my Savior that gives me peace surpassing all understanding. Enjoy—and allow your chains to be broken too so you can live a life of wisdom, mental freedom, and never-ending peace.

What a joy!

1

THE PICTURE OF AN
IDEAL FAMILY

> The beginning of my life ... a child, destined with a
> purpose ... crying all the time, scared by siblings and
> mom ... but God, Jesus, and the Holy Spirit

> Before I formed thee in the belly, I knew thee; and before
> thou camest forth out of the womb, I sanctified thee, and
> I ordained thee a prophet unto the nations.
> —Jeremiah 1:5

didn't see anything wrong with charging a nickel for penny candy. Even at the tender age of five, it seemed to make good business sense, and money was very important to me back then. That was just who I was—Bonita McAfee—a quick, bright child who could be bold. When I saw an opportunity, I went for it.

But I was also a shy, insecure kid who cried all the time. My older sisters and brothers thought it was great fun to scare me, and it turned me into a fidgety little thing, nervously pulling out my own hair. Whereas all my sisters had beautiful long hair, mine was short and patchy. Even at the age of five, I knew I was the ugliest of the bunch. Getting held back once in kindergarten only made things worse. I started acting out, even bullying other kids.

Yet despite all that, or maybe because of it, I was the leader of the pack of our little group—my two sisters Angie and Chris and my cousins, Yvonne, Doris, and Sheila. We'd spend long carefree days in our "playhouse," an abandoned garage that squatted across the street from our own home in Eau Claire, Michigan. I was the one in charge of all the candy and the money, establishing myself as the unofficial leader. That ended abruptly one unhappy day when my dad discovered I was gouging all the kids and shut me down. The spirits of mammon and power were controlling me at a very young age, and my dad knew it.

There were seven of us McAfee kids—Willie, Clotee, little Alice ("Renee"), Jerry, Chris, Angie, and me. My mother, Alice, had a glorious voice but never traveled or pursued a career, choosing to raise us kids instead. Like Mom, my older sister "little Alice" could sing and act too. She was a born entertainer, with a golden voice like Aretha Franklin's.

When I was five, I would mimic them, belting out tunes around the house like Stevie Wonder's "All in Love is Fair," Aretha Franklin's "I'm Climbing High Mountains Trying to Get Home," Michael Jackson's "Who's Loving You," Gladys Knight's "Neither One of Us," and Barbara Streisand's "Evergreen." By the age of seven, I was a strong lead singer.

We lived on McAfee Hill in Eau Claire, Michigan, near the fruit belt, where pigs were slaughtered in November.

Our grandmother, Alberta McAfee, would burn the skin off the pigs in big black kettles to render the lard we used for cooking biscuits and fried chicken, then give us kids the crackling to savor. As a child, I felt that God must really love me to give me a life like this, even if I did have short hair.

It seemed to me we had a family out of a dream, like the ones I'd seen on TV. My father worked hard to give us food, shelter, and clothing so that we would want for nothing. He not only provided for us but also for other family members and anyone else on McAfee Hill. He owned McAfee Construction, a commercial construction company, and he built houses and churches, along with working a full-time factory job at Auto Specialty in Benton Harbor, Michigan. He was a faithful churchgoer, first at Macedonia Community Church, which he built in Eau Claire, then at New Bethel Missionary Baptist Church in Benton Harbor, Michigan, where he built a new addition onto the church. He was also a brilliant businessperson, all with just an eighth-grade education.

On Sunday mornings, we'd arrive at church at 9 a.m., in time for Sunday school and services, and then spend the day there participating in an afternoon program and not leaving BTU (Baptist Training Union) until sometimes as late as 6 p.m. As a child, I couldn't understand why we had to stay there so long, not realizing at the time that our church was a hospital as well.

However, beyond that, something else bothered me, though back then I couldn't put my finger on it. As an adult, I would come to recognize that hypocrisy is what seemed to nag at me: all those people spending hours upon hours there being "good Christians," whereas all the while, outside of church, rumor had it that they were sleeping with someone else's spouse or being unkind to neighbors and "friends." Too many of these folks believed they were spiritual, but their lifestyles didn't represent a real relationship with God. I was seeing principalities in real time and didn't have the wisdom or knowledge to understand the flesh and spiritual side of us all.

In Matthew 22:37–39, we read, "Jesus replied: 'Love the Lord your God with all your heart and with all your soul and with all your mind." This is the first and greatest commandment. And the second is similar: "Love your neighbor as yourself." Clearly, Jesus intended that we put our Father God before all else and then love our neighbors and treat them with kindness and compassion. A person can spend long hours in a church, posing as a Christian, but if they do not heed these two basic commandments, then they are simply not "good Christians" and are being led by adversarial spirits rather than the Holy Spirit.

Eventually, my dad became a deacon of the church and my mom became active in the youth department and choir. Mom was the epitome of wisdom and glamour, in addition to being wonderfully talented, and was recognized by many as one of the greatest singers in the city. When Alice McAfee sang, she could bring the house down, such was the strong anointing on her voice. She was truly a woman of God.

Through my own trials, I've come to understand the power of God and assurance of His presence when a person is in pain and searching for Him. My mom knew that too. She knew it then and she continues to know it to this very day.

As far back as I can remember, my mom and dad displayed a true love for each other, but like any married couple, they had issues with one another. When they'd fight, I'd ask that if they ever decided to divorce, to wait until I'd graduated high school. I was very close with my parents, but as the years passed, I began to see a change in our home, though I wouldn't understand why for some time.

My dad worked very hard at his jobs and would come in the house at the end of the day with a frown on his face every day. Meanwhile, my mom cooked breakfast, lunch, and dinner for the family until she started to work at Memorial Hospital in Benton Harbor, and even then, she still made us breakfast and dinner daily.

Mom taught us girls how to cook, clean, and do laundry. She was always available to talk, but I didn't take advantage of that very often. I was a different child, a middle child in my own world. It was a world of loneliness and insecurities at a young age. I held all my feelings inside. When God has a calling on your life, every demon will try to hinder your path any way he can.

When I was very young, my dad would take us kids out, sometimes to look over the twenty-six acres of land we owned and of which he was so proud. Other times, he'd take us into town to Burger King to buy us lunch. My dad was an amazing father, uncle, friend, and neighbor.

During those years, our Christmases were like any kid's dream come true. Every one of us seven McAfee children had a designated area where my parents would pile up our gifts and toys. And the generosity didn't end there, often extending to other family members and neighbors, with gifts and toys as well as food. My folks would go on a spending spree, buying everything from bikes to Easy-Bake Ovens to big dolls with long golden hair.

I have great parents, I'd think.

Our parents were so loving and caring; they taught us the meaning of giving as well as the foundation of Jesus, even in the midst of the enemy stealing his way into our family structure.

I guess I never understood why I had dreams and visions of being in the entertainment industry or on TV all glammed up, but at the age of nine, God led me, and I began to fix myself up. I started to comb my own hair and put pretty ribbons in it. And it was at this age that I met Kevin, the boy I would one day marry.

Me at age 9—with pretty ribbons in my hair

But the biggest change in my life came at the age of ten, when my dear sweet mother forced me to do something I never thought I'd do.

2

SECRETS REVEALED

The chapter in my life I had to embrace … Kindergarten …
but God

Submit yourselves therefore to God. Resist the devil, and
he will flee from you.

—James 4:7

At the age of ten, God used my gifts and talents to keep a certain part of me proud of myself. He did this work through my mother, who forced me to sing in the beginner's choir under the directorship of Reverend Jerry Lott at the New Bethel Missionary Baptist church in Benton Harbor, Michigan. My mother was the youth director at church, and she knew I could sing. Because she forced me to be a part of the choir, I had no other choice but to push past my shyness and insecurities and feel comfortable with singing in front of people.

I sang primarily at church and, at a very early age, received standing ovations. Folks said I had a strong voice, so I continued singing in church and even performed in talent shows at school and other special engagements. It was truly a part of me, and though I didn't understand the magnitude of its importance at that time, I knew it was something that just made my heart beat. I could sing, and that's when I'd feel amazing as a person.

This newfound confidence began to shine through my life in other ways. I excelled in gym class, practicing almost every day, racing the boys in the family down McAfee Hill, coming in first almost every time. God began to show me other ways I could make good choices and use my talents. I was captain of the cheerleading squad and was one of the fastest runners in school, voted best athlete and even best dressed my senior year. In eleventh and twelfth grade, I began taking college courses, was on the National Honor Society, and was published in the *Who's Who Among American High School Students.* At the same time, I won a singing contest in our talent show at school.

Times were good at school and at church, but for reasons I couldn't explain, things had changed at home and my feelings of trust and security began to fade.

As First Lady of the church where my father was pastor, my mother served her members well. She was a strong, anointed singing woman of God, and every day, through her deeds, she showed the love of Christ. She would cook and serve dinners at the church; buy clothes for some of the church members; and teach women whose only desire was to sing the purpose of their gift and to embrace it, giving them songs and practicing with them. (Many of them still sing in that church to this very day.) Mother just smiled and loved them all. Folks in the church loved her back, not just because she held the title of First Lady but because she had a heart to serve the Lord and her church and did both with passion and commitment, always going above and beyond the call of duty. My mom allowed the Holy Spirit to lead her in working with people.

For years, I felt the tension between my parents, but their relationship confused me. As a child, I witnessed the love they had for each other as I sat outside their bedroom door. Yet I would also see behavior that started to draw them apart. The spirit in our home was changing.

My father and mother started to experience principalities and powers in high places because they committed their lives to Jesus. They were the perfect couple, loving Jesus and leading their kids in the same direction. But the adversarial spirits began working in ways that went beyond their abilities to see God.

Philippians 2:5 (KJV) says, "Let this mind be in you, which is also in Christ Jesus."

My parents' minds seemed to start drifting into a mold dictated by the world and the environment around them.

My father was a husband, and my mother was a wife with seven

7

children. It became difficult to see God amid the clouds rising at the core of the union God had ordained between them.

The Bible tells us in John 16:33, "These things I have spoken unto you, that in me ye might have peace. In the world ye shall have tribulations: but be of good cheer; I have overcome the world."

Satan will stop at nothing to get us off the path God has placed us upon. God ordained marriage as a sacred union, but I know now what I didn't understand then—it's a lot of work. I know now that an abundance of sinful influences attract our minds and eyes. If we're unable to die to pride and flesh, eventually those influences cause our relationships to suffer. They can consume even the strongest of Christians.

"With persuasive words she led him astray; she seduced him with her smooth talk. All at once he followed her like an ox going to the slaughter, like a deer stepping into a noose, till an arrow pierces his liver, like a bird darting into a snare, little knowing it will cost him his life" (Proverbs 7:21–23).

The word of God must be so engrained in our minds, hearts, and souls that it would be very difficult for the adversary to have his way with us. Sometimes we're so consumed that we can't even see what's coming at us. My dad and mom's relationship was being targeted, and they couldn't even see through the clouds covering them. Their spiritual eyes were being blinded by the way of the world. It became difficult to turn back.

My parents' marriage began to suffer because of their minds and hearts being consumed in a toxic environment that was created for them. And because of this, I found myself becoming distrustful and angry toward men.

Eventually, my parents couldn't hold on any longer, and we witnessed firsthand what sin can do when people are unable to stay in the will of God. Strong spirits will wage a powerful battle in the flesh when the minds of people are unable to stay focused on Christ.

During times of confusion, it can be very difficult to understand that God is using us for a higher purpose. We all are flesh, and we will sin.

Psalms 51:5 tells us, "Behold, I was shapen in iniquity; and in sin did my mother conceive me." We were born in sin, and that was the purpose for Jesus dying and sending the comforter, the Holy Spirit, to lead and guide us daily.

Generational curses are very real and travel throughout families. They can only be broken with a mind determined to allow the Holy Spirit to lead. It's nearly impossible any other way. There are times in relationships when pride gets so heavy that before long, a family is destroyed and children are left trying to figure out how to pick up the pieces. I feel my dad and mom were subjected to this and just couldn't find their way back.

In fact, my parents' behavior started to change right before my eyes. It's painful as a child to see two people so in love lose sight of their beginning. The world that surrounds godly people is orchestrated to keep division and hopelessness in the family structure, causing it to fail. We become so involved in the matters of the world that we lose sight of God and His purpose for creating us.

There is no one on this planet who can escape trials and tribulations. We all will have the opportunity to exercise our faith in Jesus and allow Him to fix our relationships as we experience difficulties beyond our control. However, our challenge will always be between focusing on ourselves (pride) and allowing the Holy Spirit to lead, guide, and direct us in the true path of righteousness.

It is amazing how enticing sin can be and how our lives can change overnight. My parents' marriage—and by extension, our family—was being jeopardized as part of our mutual journey to get closer to Jesus.

The adversarial spirits had made their way into our home. Our family and all our lives would never be the same.

3

FACING REALITIES: MY GRADUATION AND MOVING ON

God promised me He would never leave me alone, and He didn't.

Fear thou not; for I am with thee: be not dismayed; for I am thy God: I will strengthen thee; yea, I will help thee; yea, I will uphold thee with the right hand of my righteousness.
—Isaiah 41:10

ur pasts and individuals who are hurting and looking for love in the wrong places can affect us all. I don't feel people get married and have children just to hurt each other and their families. Pain and hurt from our pasts due to an absent father or mother or just bad counsel can interrupt any married couple trying to live their lives for Jesus. The Bible tells us in John 16:33, "These things I have spoken unto you, that in me ye might have peace. In the world ye shall have tribulation: but be of good cheer; I have overcome the world."

Hurt people hurt people, and sometimes the pains of our pasts drive us into areas that can be very unhealthy. The ways of life can get so dark and lonely, even when people are around, and God is the only one who can see us through these difficult times. Marriage is bringing two imperfect people together to create one union, and God must be the head of that union, not the tail. We all will be tried in the fire, and Jesus left a road map for us, but there are times when we take detours on the road and suffer as a result.

God has since allowed me to experience and see what happens when we decide to feed the flesh instead of the Spirit, which lives inside each one of us. It's hard to get back to shore when Satan has convinced you that you are not worthy of Jesus's love. It pains me even now to think about it.

The consequences of our actions not only hurt us but affected everyone around us as well. After twenty-seven years of marriage, seven kids, five years of pastoring for my father and five years as First Lady for my mom, the marriage ended. My wonderful parents' relationship couldn't withstand the various storms.

I now realize the importance of having positive people around you who love and fear the Lord to give good counsel.

Proverbs 11:14 says, "Where no counsel is, the people fall: but in the multitude of counsellors there is safety."

My mom and all three of us girls left for Los Angeles that summer after my high school graduation. My parents had in fact waited to split until after commencement, and I realized that we had spoken this thing into existence. For us, many dreams had shattered but not all were broken. The family was devastated.

I moved with my mom and siblings from Michigan to LA but returned in the fall to attend college in Grand Rapids.

Later that summer, I returned from Los Angeles to get ready for college, accompanied by my sister Chris, and my cousins, Von, Doris, and Brenda. We had so much freedom, but at the same time, we were experiencing so much pain. We missed my parents and the way it felt to be one family all together.

I'd completed eleventh and twelfth grade and attended Lake Michigan College early, despite having been held back. The house in which I'd been raised had been a sanctuary of sorts. Now that house was newly remodeled after a fire had destroyed it months earlier. Gone were my state track trophies, certificates, and medals; the mementos that were like snapshots of my life were nothing more than ash now, including pictures and letters I'd received from Kevin all the way back to when we were just ten years old. All of it had been destroyed. And in that sense, a home that had once been a sanctuary for so many was gone.

Still, my cousins all visited the new house that took its place, and I would invite my Kevin to stop by too. The life we had known was over, and another chapter had begun without our consent. I was feeling a tremendous amount of rejection and pain, and that came out in the form of major rebellion.

We'd party. I'd cook, and Kevin and I would have a blast together. We were like zombies, dead to this life, our home like a *House of the Dead* where principalities had set up camp.

As a high-achieving teen, I'd never been tempted to try marijuana before. But now, sensing my pain and the spirit in which I was operating, was not positive. Suddenly, the thought of using drugs no longer bothered me.

The first time I smoked dope, I went behind my parents' house. Though all that had taken place devastated me, I still respected my parents enough not to do drugs in their home. I took my first puff at the age of eighteen, thinking it was no big deal. I was okay for a while and felt quite normal, but eventually I began to feel an unfamiliar feeling that was completely unlike my usual self. It was as if another spirit had taken over my mind and body. I ended up cussing out everyone in the house. A feeling of numbness overtook my brain, which was wonderfully liberating.

> Why should you be beaten anymore? Why do you persist in rebellion? Your whole head is injured, your whole heart afflicted.
>
> —Isaiah 1: 5–6

I didn't care about anything. I was totally zoned out and decided that this was life's best-kept secret. I was in so much pain, and smoking weed numbed that pain. Every time I came down from a high, I would smoke again, and the pain would just vanish into the air, like the smoke I exhaled from my lungs. I pulled away from both my mother and my father. I couldn't trust getting close to them again.

Adding to my pain was the fact that my mother and sisters were not home to take me to my first day of college. My dad was in Michigan but completely devastated over the loss of his family. He was confused and hurt because he did love my mother and us kids, but life has a way of taking multiple unexpected turns. Instead of family, my dad arranged for Linetta Smith, one of our church members, to take me to college.

I started school at Davenport Business College in Grand Rapids, Michigan, with the intent to make healthy choices for my life, and to some degree, I did. I completed all my homework, but my lifestyle was something else.

I continued along a path of self-destruction. I had major trust issues and didn't know if I would ever have the faith again to trust that I could spend my life with a man. I thought a man would leave me, as I felt my dad had. Though I'd grown up in a two-parent home, there had still been issues between my mom and dad. It's hard to make logical decisions when so many of your thoughts and emotions are a product of the environment in which you've been raised. Sometimes it's hard to understand how much and in what ways it does affect you.

Kevin wanted to be my only boyfriend and to get married. Whenever he'd bring it up, I'd panic and my inner voice would shout, *Are you kidding me! Do you really think I can trust you after witnessing a seemingly perfect marriage crumble after twenty-seven years?*

I'd tell Kevin he should go on his way and experience being with multiple women so that when we did come together, he wouldn't say, "Wish I woulda /coulda …" I was a total mess.

I was so broken that I just couldn't allow any man to have me to himself. I couldn't commit. I didn't trust love or men at all. I'd often think, *I really have acquired a warped outlook on life. Jesus, please help me.*

I attended church all the time, but I didn't seek God's face in this season of my life. I didn't feel I had direction or application of how I could access God. I didn't understand.

> He writes the same way in all his letters, speaking in them of these matters. His letters contain some things that are hard to understand, which ignorant and unstable people distort, as they do the other scriptures, to their own destruction.
>
> Therefore, dear friends, since you have been forewarned, be on your guard so that you may not be carried away by

the error of the lawless and fall from your secure position. But grow in the grace and knowledge of our Lord and Savior, Jesus Christ. To Him be glory both now and forever! Amen.

—2 Peter 3:16–18

I was simply intent on self-destruction and destruction of others with whom I came into contact. I was so mad and outraged about my parents' divorce.

It was like a death, but I was living. I spent time rebellion shopping as though I were wealthy. My dad, being the great father he was, sent me as much money as I needed and some I didn't need. He was the kind of father any little girl would dream of and be lucky to have—a bighearted giver known for helping family and anyone in need. I really didn't know what I was going to do without him and my mom being in the same home with me.

After I started college, I experienced many vicissitudes. My family was the stability in my life, and suddenly things had changed. I was in a new city, a new environment, with roommates, new teachers, and professors. My life seemed like a nightmare from a horror movie. I felt like the main character waiting for the movie to end.

I was furious about this intrusion of what I know now were principalities and powers in high places taking over a little girl's world of love and happiness … her family. My sisters and brothers were so protective of us three little girls, Chris, Angie, and me. There was nothing we needed that they didn't try to extend to us. We all were going through our own personal journey during our parents' divorce.

Various situations caused some upheaval in a family that was already fractured. My father and mother were going through their own battles in the spiritual realm, making sure that we kids and everyone around could still see the God they served.

My family went through some major changes as well as opportunities God was giving us to allow Him to reign in our lives as never before. Of course, we couldn't see what he was doing, but God was always working behind the scenes for my family. "For my thoughts are not your thoughts, neither are your ways my ways, saith the Lord. For as the heavens are higher than the earth, so are my ways higher than your ways, and my thoughts than your thoughts" (Isaiah 55:8–9).

Finally, my mother called a family meeting, something she often did to restore unity and harmony to our family. She has always been such a great mom and woman of God. She shared how awesome of a dad our father was and said we were to look to God during this time of transition, always remembering that we wanted for nothing. She told us that we were to trust God in what He had allowed to happen and it all would work for our good.

My time in college became a bridge to helping me cope with the divorce of my parents. I began to embrace living in a great apartment with interesting roommates. Instead of working hard at school, I focused on getting just enough done to get by and spent the rest of my time partying my pain away. I had my first experiences with drinking on one particular night, guzzling down a concoction of vodka, gin, and red punch, which so disabled me that I couldn't function that evening or even the next morning.

I chose to live a life of total freedom and found myself doing fashion shows and getting involved in school in order to feel worthy and proud of myself, despite my internal struggles. I shopped a lot and was one of the best-dressed students in college. (Thank God for Gantos Boutique.) Shopping and fashion always seemed to ease my pain and make me look and feel good. And if I couldn't feel good on the inside, at least I wanted to look good on the outside.

I was studying to become a legal secretary, but my grades went south quickly that first semester. The college expelled students by the hundreds if they weren't making it academically, and I didn't want to get thrown out of school. In addition to my emotional turmoil, I wasn't very interested in my major, so I switched to studying fashion and merchandising. My grades went up immediately, and I discovered my focus and area of interest. At the end of my time there, I graduated with a fashion and merchandising degree, despite all I was going through.

Commencement was a celebration, with both my mom and dad in attendance. I drove away from campus in a yellow Ford Mustang that my father had given me as a congratulatory gift, steering myself toward LA, one of the fashion capitals of the world.

Things were finally going to change for the better.

CONTROL MY MIND AFFIRMATIONS

I'm pausing at this point in my story to share something important with my readers. Our midlife crises, as well as many other things, can make us think all kinds of things that are just not true about our personal circumstances. This can drive us to make unhealthy choices. Our minds are attacked, and as a result, everything around us starts to fall apart. Neither my dad and mom, nor Kevin and I, had any desire for our family to be targeted. We all wanted to be married for sixty years or more. Our hearts and spirits were willing, but our minds and flesh were weakened. This is not unlike what so many others are dealing with today. Please know that it all starts in the mind. We must think and speak with positivity because we become what we think and speak.

If you're experiencing any kind of negative thoughts and pain because of a divorce, death, or other loss, this is when your mind must become consumed with the word of God and positive thinking.

The following are what I call "Control My Mind Affirmations." I use them daily to keep my heart, my head, and my spirit in line with Jesus. I encourage you to use them as well—and even to write your own in the journal pages that follow. My story continues after the journal pages.

Thank you, Jesus, for keeping my mind on you today, Holy Spirit.
Help me, Jesus, keep my mind, heart, and soul focused only on you today.
Guide my mind today, Jesus.
Control every thought, Holy Spirit.
Please, Jesus, help me keep my mind on you, in spite of what others do.
Deliver my mind from negative thoughts.
Give me your mind, Lord, that praises in the midst of darkness.
Be the light unto the path of my mind today, Jesus.
Lord, guide my mind beyond my circumstances and what I can see.
Jesus, keep my mind only on you today.
Thank you, Jesus, for freeing my mind at Calvary, setting me free today.
Thank you, Jesus, for your blood that flows through my mind, body, and soul.
Thank you, Jesus, for staying in control of my mind today.

Please guide my mind, my thoughts, and my tongue today, Jesus.
Help me remember not to forget, Jesus, whose I am today.
Thank you for being a mind-regulating, heart-fixing, company-keeping God.
Thank you, Jesus, for being the Great I Am.

Journal Pages
Write Your Own Affirmations

Journal Pages

Journal Pages

Journal Pages

Journal Pages

Journal Pages

Journal Pages

4

FOR THE GOOD OF THOSE WHO LOVE HIM

The turning point ... I talked about and dreamed of being in the music and entertainment industry ... On the road with Stevie Wonder ... God planned it His way.

And we know that in all things God works for the good of those who love Him, who have been called according to His purpose.

—Romans 8:28

od took my fractured family and began to heal and make us whole again. Allowing the Holy Spirit to work through her, my mom extended an olive branch of peace to my dad and his new family, including them in an invitation to come to Los Angeles and join the entire family in celebrating Christmas that year. In this way, my mom was loving people into the submission of God and not allowing the spirits of bitterness, hate, and division to keep us out of the will of God.

But that wasn't out of the ordinary for my mother, Alice McAfee. She was a real woman of God who truly loved and did her best to live the life of Jesus. She continues to be so to this day. She is everything a First Lady should be, with her focus on God, prayer, love and family. My mom assessed the situation and determined that there was no way she was ever going to allow the enemy to block the relationship she or any of her family had with our Father in heaven.

She would always say of folks who brought trials to our door, "I'm headed somewhere, and they will not get in the way of my getting to heaven."

My mother never talked negatively about my father or his new family. After all, my dad had been a good father and a great provider. We all sometimes find ourselves trying to do good and stay on the path of Christ. But principalities are right there to keep us focused on the world, in spite of the level of Jesus in our lives.

> For the good that I would I do not: but the evil which I would not, that I do. Now if I do that I would not, it is no more I that do it, but sin that dwelleth in me. I find then a law, that, when I would do good, evil is present with me. For I delight in the law of God after the inward man: But I see another law in my members, warring against the law of my mind, and bringing me into captivity to the law of sin which is in my members. O wretched man that I am! who shall deliver me from the body of this death? I thank God through Jesus Christ our Lord. So then with the mind I myself serve the law of God; but with the flesh the law of sin
>
> —Romans 7:19–25

> At the end of your life you will groan when your flesh and body are spent. You will say, "How I hated discipline! How my heart spurned correction! I would not obey my teachers or listen to my instructors. I have come to the brink of utter ruin in the midst of the whole assembly
>
> —Proverbs 5:11–14

I understand now that it is impossible to say I believe in Jesus yet not take Him at His word. I realize that we are all at war every day with the inner man, trying to stay on the righteous path, yet Satan's job is to try to overthrow the purpose God has for us on a daily basis.

For me, life seemed to be on an upswing. After graduating from Davenport Business College with a degree in fashion and merchandising, I moved to Los Angeles to pursue my dreams and be near my family. Making the most of God's gifts, in 1985, I formed a singing group called RARE (Rebuilding Awareness, Reaffirming Education) with my sister Angela and a friend named Tracy. We performed all over Los Angeles and Sacramento, singing to appreciative audiences and touching the lives of students and families. Folks compared my voice to the likes of the great Mahalia Jackson, as well as Shirley Caesar, Yolanda Adams, and Anita Baker. Our goal was always to create music that raised awareness of social and emotional issues that were important, such as education, self-esteem, and faith. This outlet became a saving grace for my spirit and heart.

It was during this time that our focus and our fortunes changed. In addition to composing and singing, I had always had a passion for making women feel good about themselves. With my background in merchandising and fashion, I knew what clothing would work and look good on women, especially those who were full-figured. Combining my efforts with the gifts of my sister Angela, whose charisma and charm made her a talented networker, we met Lula Mae Hardaway, the mother of legendary singer-songwriter Stevie Wonder.

What followed was a whirlwind of excitement. Ms. Hardaway became my first celebrity private wardrobe client, whose son just happened to be a celebrity as well. The clothing we carried came from a fashion line out of Italy, and Lula Mae looked like a million bucks in them. We'd visit her in her home in Woodland Hills, California, and in downtown Chicago, which led to an introduction to her famous son. And because Stevie was in transition at the time, we landed his wardrobe account, creating custom-made costumes for him, his band, and his backup singers. My older sister Clotee even designed the outfit that he wore to his induction into the Rock & Roll Hall of Fame, and I was right there to experience the celebration with my favorite celebrity artist. This was truly the beginning of something that would have seemed improbable to a red dirt–eating little country girl like me from Eau Claire, Michigan. But there was more to come and experience in the world of music and the entertainment industry.

New York was one of our first tours as the new stylist and design team for Stevie Wonder. We stayed at The Plaza Hotel near Central Park, owned at the time by Donald Trump. He and Ivana came to one of the shows and told us how great Stevie was looking. We were only to be in New York for one week, with Stevie performing at Radio City Music Hall. In the end, we spent five weeks there, shopping all up and down Fifth Avenue. What a major transition God had allowed to take place in my life during a tough time internally. For the first time in my life, I paid five hundred dollars for several pairs of boots. Wow, what a real treat! I had only dreamed of this lifestyle, and it was actually happening.

From Monte Carlo to Brunei (where I had my own villa and sat at a table eating with Sting) to Spain to Italy, we toured with Stevie and the band. In Australia, we visited a beautiful zoo. We toured Japan, France, and Britain, where celebrities like Chaka Khan, Cindy Lauper, and Boyz II Men attended a birthday party concert for Stevie. We visited many more countries as well as various cities in the United States. I met Celine Dion and her husband at the American Music Awards, as well as Bob Hope, Elizabeth Taylor, and Mary Tyler Moore in Palm Springs. The Soul Train Awards was power-packed with celebrities like Don King, Whitney Houston, Pattie LaBelle, and more. It all seemed like a dream, but it wasn't. God had given me a kid-in-a- candy-store life, allowing me to see just how much He loved me in spite me of feeling my world had ended.

I got to experience what it felt like to sit at the piano with Stevie and harmonize with him on the song of his that I'd been singing since I was a little girl: "All Is Fair in Love." He even honored me by critiquing the first song I'd ever written as a solo artist, "Just Me."

JUST ME

Music and Lyrics by Bonita McAfee Mitchell

First verse:

I've gone through life unsure of who I am or what I should be;
Attached to people and things were just a part of my insecurity.
I now realize happiness inside is the key to my life;
It can't be compromised. Now I can see just me.

Hook:

Just me, me and only me.
Just me, just me, me and only me.
Just me, just me, now I can see
I've got to first believe in me

"Believe in first and only me" (Stevie's input)

Second verse:

The joy I feel sometimes inside my soul, it's really real.
It comes from serving people, having faith in dreams,
taking control
Of my destiny; it's all up to me.
I've got to accept who I am
and the gifts that have been given to me.
Now I can see just me.

Hook:

Just me, me and only me.
Just me, just me, me and only me.
Just me, just me, now I can see
I've got to first believe in me.

"Believe in first and only me" (Stevie's input)

Bridge:

One of the greatest powers I can now embrace
Is to accept the reflection of my own faith.
The light is now on, and the truth I can finally see—
The greatest gift in life is to learn to love me.

Hook:

Just me, me and only me.
Just me, just me, me and only me.
Just me, just me, now I can see
I've got to first believe in me.

"Believe in First and Only Me"
(Stevie's input)

The final concert we attended in South Africa after the end of apartheid was one at which Stevie performed to celebrate Nelson Mandela's eightieth birthday. Michael Jackson and practically every major celebrity attended. While I was in South Africa, I had the opportunity to tour the outback, seeing big elephants, tall giraffes, hippos, and more. Johannesburg was the most beautiful city I'd ever seen in my life. It was all a fitting and emotional conclusion to a memorable time in my life that I will never forget, and I am thankful God counted me worthy.

I often think about what would have happened if I had allowed depression, principalities, and every other hindering spirit to stop me. What would have become of these amazing opportunities with which God had blessed me? I had to keep moving and trusting in what I couldn't see or feel. God stayed in control. It doesn't matter what life brings at us—if we are willing to follow the word of Jesus and His powerful Holy Spirit, we can never go wrong.

God was setting me up for a greater purpose than I'd ever imagined. He allowed me the experiences to travel and meet all these celebrities because He knew I would share my testimony, letting youth and families know just how powerful He really is when we decide never to give up on Him. I became a counselor on the road with the singers and band. God was working with me even then, and I didn't realize it.

However, like most things in life, change is inevitable. R.A.R.E. disbanded, and I found myself alone again. But still the Lord continued to feed me with inspiration, giving me the lyrics and melodies to new songs, while prospering my wardrobe business. The number of clients increased, and my fan base grew.

5

BY MYSELF BUT NEVER TRULY ALONE

What a change … Kevin meets me in Los Angeles

The husband must fulfill his duty to his wife, and likewise also the wife to her husband.

—1 Corinthians 7:3

One that ruleth well his own house, having his children in subjection with all gravity …

—1 Timothy 3:4

hen I was ten years old, I told Kevin I was going to marry him one day. Then, in 1986, just fifteen years later, that's exactly what I did. It's funny how things work out sometimes, though I do believe there needs to be a definite order to things. Life events need to be lived in a logical sequence.

Kevin and I lived together before we were married, both of us working and splitting the rent. For some, cohabitating might not seem out of the ordinary, but Kevin's mother was a pastor, as was my father, so it was not the norm in our world. Yet Kevin and I thought nothing of it at the time. Now, of course, I believe that when a family is unable to follow the biblical order of things, they are headed for trouble.

We saw this firsthand in how the generational curse from our parents traveled and plagued our relationship. Biblically, I was supposed to be the helpmate, have the babies and raise them, and do what I could to support my husband. He was to take care of the home, being responsible for the bills. But we didn't play those roles, and we lost the order of the family structure.

> Unto the woman he said, I will greatly multiply thy sorrow and thy conception; in sorrow thou shalt bring forth children; and thy desire shall be to thy husband, and he shall rule over thee.
>
> And unto Adam he said, Because thou hast hearkened unto the voice of they wife, and hast eaten of the tree, of which I commanded thee, saying Thou shalt to eat of it: cursed is the ground for thy sake; in sorrow shalt thou eat of it all the days of thy life;
>
> Therefore, the Lord God sent him forth from the garden of Eden, to till the ground from whence he was taken.
> —Genesis 3:16–17, 23

Around the time that I was traveling all around the world with Stevie Wonder and R.A.R.E. had disbanded, Kevin and I had been married for about ten years. It felt to me as if there was a distance between us, and it seemed as if my husband wasn't truly loving me anymore. We separated. At the time, Kevin took our then–seven-year-old son with him. We'd agreed years earlier, even before we became parents, that if we ever did split up, Kevin would take any boy children with him and I would take any girl children with me. We'd also agreed that if we ever started fighting in front of our kids, we'd separate.

What I hadn't realized at the time and did not come to learn for a long while afterward was that my husband had encountered a situation he couldn't get out of, for about two years, and was unable to recover. I had been away traveling but could feel something was wrong. He'd been too embarrassed to share with me the details of what had transpired. Our relationship took a hit, and it was a very trying time those few years. It seemed like a lifetime. Eventually, because of Kevin's love and commitment to God, his soul was revived. We found our way back to where God had predestined us to be. I didn't know at the time that there was a calling on Kevin's life.

I listened when the Holy Spirit told me to suggest he go home to Michigan, where he loved the outdoors and visiting his family.

And then I was alone. Missing my group, separated from my husband and son, I had to trust God to give me the courage to accept my life circumstances, see Him in everything around me, and embrace my gift of singing, composing, producing, and still working with Stevie Wonder. I knew it was time to move forward.

Despite my family's absence, I knew I was never truly alone.

Journal Pages

Journal Pages

Journal Pages

Journal Pages

6

LIVING MY PURPOSE: THREAD OF HOPE RECORDS BIRTHS "I'M SAVING MYSELF"

Move back to Michigan ... Thread of Hope Records—
"I'm Saving Myself" and ISM Academy Programs ... God
creates a stream in the desert ... Major issues ... But God

Behold, I will do a new thing; now it shall spring forth;
shall ye not know it? I will even make a way in the
wilderness and rivers in the desert.

—Isaiah 43:19

Through music, RARE worked to create messages that challenged kids to think about what they were doing and what was driving them to make the decisions they were making about things like sex, drugs, depression, suicide, and abuse. Inspired by that experience, I launched my own record label, Thread of Hope (TOH) Records, with the goal of continuing to make music that prompted awareness.

In 1998, I was asked to return to my old hometown of Eau Claire, Michigan, after a popular local teen basketball player had committed suicide. Ministering to the community uncovered a new purpose and direction for my label and me.

This was the beginning of TOH Record's prevention program that addressed low self-esteem, bullying, cyberbullying, drugs, alcohol, suicide, teen pregnancy, child molestation, and violence, all through music and performing arts—"Celebrate Life & Pursue Your Dreams." The program involved kids advocating to kids through hip-hop music and dance, encouraging them to make different choices and to go after their dreams. Through a platform of music and performing arts, they could support and encourage one another while making better life choices for themselves.

A Celebrate Life & Pursue Your Dreams performance

CHERISH YOUR LIFE

Music and Lyrics by Bonita McAfee Mitchell for All Heart Publishing
Producer: Bonita McAfee Mitchell

Intro:

This song is dedicated to the families affected by people who have died from suicide. And for the people who are listening, choose life; cherish it.

First verse:

I remember those days very well,
Holding feelings inside no one could tell.
Then I started to lose the same power I used—that kept me going day by day.
Before I knew it, I became engaged
In a world full of hopelessness and rage.
Now I know what to do to try to warn and save you.
Please don't make the same mistake too. You've got to …

Chorus:

Cherish your life, no matter when times get tough.
Cherish your life. You can make it; just don't give up.
Cherish your life. Loving yourself is the key, then put your trust in thee.
You've got to …
Cherish your life. Save yourself and don't give in.
Cherish your life, even when it feels like the end.
Cherish your life; you've got the power to make it through.
Your life, your destiny, depends on you.

Second verse:

If I had to do it over again,
I would trust and I'd tell a special friend
What I had planned to do, because I felt I couldn't make it through
Life's journey, filled with hopelessness and full of pain.

I can share with you now; you need to know
You can make it anywhere you choose to go.
But the choice that I made— it led me straight to my grave
And I beg you: choose life, release the strife. You've got to

Chorus:

Cherish your life, no matter when times get tough.
Cherish your life; you can make it—just don't give up.
Cherish your life. Loving yourself is the key, then put your trust in thee.
You've got to …
Cherish your life. Save yourself and don't give in.
Cherish your life, even when it feels like the end.
Cherish your life; you've got the power to make it through.
Your life, your destiny, depends on you.

Bridge:

Dark clouds may come, and they may go,
But there's one thing I know.
After heartache and pain comes sunshine and rain
Don't give up. Someone loves and cares for you.
You've got to …

TOH Records's first artist was a beautiful, shy fifteen-year-old from Nashville, Tennessee, named Katie Giguere. Classmates were bullying her because of her size. I brought Katie in to perform for Stevie Wonder. Stevie told her that her voice was wonderful, and it completely changed her life. She went on to become a critically acclaimed chart-topping Christian music vocalist.

Katie addressed the issue of low self-esteem, and together we combined our passion for music in front of an audience of three hundred young people with a song about abstinence called "I'm Saving Myself." This performance so encouraged one eighth grader, that it convinced him not to kill himself.

"I'm Saving Myself" became our overriding theme song, and in 2002, it was the inspiration for the launch of my nonprofit I'm Saving Myself

Prevention Program (imsavingmyself.org), which helps youth and young adults find solutions through music and performing arts. To date, the program has touched the lives of more than twenty thousand young people, helping them find purpose-driven lives and teaching them to love themselves so that they will not grow up to damage the lives of innocent people as well as their own.

Through my work with I'm Saving Myself, I came to understand new things about my own life. One of the most profound discoveries was the realization that when little girls grow up without a father, they can become numb to any positive situation. While this doesn't excuse negative behavior or the years spent pursuing a male figure or idea of a father, it does shed light on the reasons some women behave in a manner that can ultimately destroy a seemingly healthy family.

I realized that there are wounded little girls in broken women and men, and as the saying goes, "Hurt people hurt people." The absence of a father dictates a lot of unhealthy behavior, and because of the pain in their lives and the love and affection that were missing from their dads, some of them set out to destroy complete families. However, they are just insecure women or men lacking a personal relationship with Jesus, finding love in the wrong places, positions, and power.

> For at the window of my house I looked out through my lattice, and I saw among the simple ones, I observed among the youths, a young man without sense, passing along the street near her corner, taking the road to her house in the twilight, in the evening, at the time of night and darkness. Then a woman comes toward him, decked out like a prostitute, wily of heart. She is loud and wayward; her feet do not stay at home; now in the street, now in the squares, and at every corner she lies in wait. She seizes him and kisses him, and with impudent face she says to him: "I had to offer sacrifices, and today I have paid my vows; so now I have come out to meet you, to seek you eagerly, and I have found you! I have decked my couch with coverings, colored spreads of Egyptian linen; I have perfumed my bed with myrrh,

aloes, and cinnamon. Come, let us take our fill of love until morning; let us delight ourselves with love."

—Proverbs 7:6–18

A lot of people lack enough God in their hearts to withstand this evil and conniving spirit, and because of that, they end up in places where most men and women fall—in bed being controlled by sexual tricks and powers from another world. Only our God in heaven can control our lives, but first we must allow Him to use us by coming into our hearts and minds.

This would be something I would need to cling to and remember in the days to come.

7

BECOMING THE FIRST LADY: MY ROLE AND COMMITMENT TO GOD

Humility and Forgiveness

Humble yourselves therefore under the mighty hand of God, that He may exalt you in due time. Casting all your care upon Him; for He careth for you.

—1 Peter 5:6–7

Take heed to yourselves: If thy brother trespasses against thee, rebuke him; and if he repent, forgive him.

—Luke 17:3

Pastor and First Lady

I n 2002, I became the First Lady of the Mt. Zion Missionary Baptist church under the leadership of my husband, Pastor Kevin Duane Mitchell, Sr. The role of First Lady in a Baptist Church is a position of honor that's given when your husband is called to pastor a church, but I feel the position must be earned.

A First Lady is expected to keep her husband and family lifted up in prayer, serve her church, and its members by demonstrating the love of Christ. Sadly, it doesn't always turn out that way. Too often, if she's not rooted in the Word, a First Lady will abuse her power and focus her efforts on making herself, rather than God, the center of attention. A First Lady like that can often turn people away from a church instead of drawing them in, even if the church is a hospital filled with sick people striving to be healed by the words of God, taught by the pastor. This is not an easy position. After all, being a Jesus-loving Christian is a job that takes denying the flesh daily, so the Holy Spirit can guide our minds, hearts, and souls throughout the day.

While I was not always the most traditional First Lady, I did work with the choir and the church members as if they were my family. This is what I saw my mother do during her five years as a First Lady. Meanwhile, my real family continued to be a source of difficulty for me.

My family was broken up, living in various states, and that was a difficult situation for me. I didn't realize then that when God allows things to happen in our lives, He gives us the opportunity to get closer to Him. It was also very comforting to know that everything that goes on in our lives must go through Him first. Romans 8:28 tells us, "And we know that in all things God works for the good of those who love Him, who have been called according to His purpose." And He had done exactly that.

As for me, during the first years of my husband acting as pastor of our church, the Holy Spirit directed me to go to my father and his new First Lady and ask them if they were aware of the little girl whose life had been torn apart. The girl to whom the Spirit referred was not their last child. It was me.

I realized that I had been holding unforgiveness in my heart and it would be impossible for me to have a pure relationship with Jesus while dealing in pride and unforgiveness. Matthew 6:14–16 tells us, "For if you forgive men their trespasses, your heavenly Father will also forgive you. But if you do not forgive men their trespasses, neither will your Father forgive your trespasses." I was in so much pain, and I needed to be able to access the comfort of Jesus inside me.

Therefore, I went to them both as that broken child that still lived inside me and told them I had been scarred and that I felt my world had been shattered by the divorce of my parents. With humility, I explained how the relationship had fractured the unity and bond of the family, as well as how it was affecting me. And by doing as the Holy Spirit directed, I discovered something I hadn't known before: they were broken too.

> The sacrifices of God are a broken spirit; a broken and
> contrite heart, O God, you will not despise.
> —Psalms 51:17

I didn't understand that God uses completely broken people to bring glory to Himself.

I asked them if they had asked God to forgive them. You see, the Holy Spirit told me that He was only concerned about our salvation and I had to be obedient to that end, even though it was hard. Both said they had asked for God's forgiveness, and it was a sign of relief for me knowing that my only concern was my obedience to the Holy Spirit. I left their house feeling a major weight had been lifted with a sense of freedom, as well as much compassion for the two of them. God didn't stop loving and supporting me when I made mistakes. He wrapped me closer in His arms as I learned to lean more on Him during my times of despair.

I feel that every child who has experienced divorce goes through some of the same issues with which I was dealing. I refused to allow it to keep me in a dark, bitter, and defeated state. I loved Jesus and my parents too much to let it happen.

Do I love them? Yes. Do I love what God allowed? No. Do I trust God when He says in Romans 8:28, "All things work together for the good of those who love Him and are called according to His purpose"? I certainly do.

I've gone through so many storms in my life, but Jesus, in His infinite wisdom, has brought me through each one so that I might come forth with my testimony. This became even more apparent to me when what followed next in my life made me feel that I was losing my mind.

For years, I'd watched my mother stick by my father as First Lady. Trying always to follow her example, I did all the same things for my husband that she had done for my father. I cooked, cleaned, and was ever-present and supportive of him. Then five years after Kevin became pastor, he told me that his heart had fled from me and he needed some time to himself. What a blow! Was I waiting for someone to wake me out of my dream? Unfortunately, I was facing what had happened to my mother!

When someone you love dearly quite suddenly tells you something like this, you are simply devastated. After all, his father had left his mother when he was just five years old, and of course, my own parents had divorced after twenty-seven years of marriage. Kevin and I had planned to be together forever.

Me, Kevin, and our son

I felt as if I'd been dropped into a big black hole. The Holy Spirit took control of my mind in the midst of my pain. He led me to call on the powerful name of Jesus and begin reading about His life and all He had suffered just so that I could live and be an example through my own suffering. In Acts 9:16, Jesus said, "For I will show him how great things he must suffer for my name's sake." I had to acknowledge that the one and only Savior was going to see me through this most devastating season of my life. There is power in the name of Jesus.

Happier times

I DECREE THE POWER IN YOUR NAME, JESUS

Your name is holy, Jesus.
There's salvation in your name, Jesus.
There's peace in your name, Jesus.
There's love in your name, Jesus.
There's deliverance in your name, Jesus.
There's healing in your name, Jesus.
There's power in your name, Jesus.
There's protection in your name, Jesus.
There's grace and mercy in your name, Jesus.
There's forgiveness in your name, Jesus.
There's miracle in your name, Jesus.
The impossible is in your name, Jesus.
At the mention of your name, Jesus, demons must flee.
For your name's sake, Jesus, there is suffering.
You're my everything, Jesus.
You're everything I need, Jesus.
You're the bright and morning star, Jesus.
You are a mender of marriages and relationships, Jesus.
You can do anything but fail, Jesus.
I'm counting on you to see me through, Jesus.

8

WHERE DO I GO FROM HERE?

Do I trust my feelings or do I trust Jesus and His word? Do I become self-centered in what I feel my husband shared about not loving me, or do I go into battle mode with the word of God, allowing the Holy Spirit to lead, guide, and direct my path? Do I believe? Do I have faith and trust in Jesus and in all He has done for me?

For we wrestle not against flesh and blood, but against principalities, against powers, against the rulers of the darkness of this world, against spiritual wickedness in high places.

—Ephesians 6:12

od would not allow me to be completely consumed by the darkness and depression that threatened to envelop me. Instead, God put me in worker mode, helping me to fight the dark spirit with the light of His Word.

I turned to the Lord as I never had before, soaking up the Word. What I didn't understand then (but would be revealed to me later) was that God was building up our ministries so that we could offer a greater testimony about Him. He was using all the painful circumstances in Kevin's and my life to give it a platform for just how good He is.

Kevin was an unbelievably gifted teacher and pastor. But what I couldn't understand then was how he could know God so well, how could he teach others that God can do all things, yet not trust God to fix our marriage? If he wanted it to be repaired, he needed to believe that it could be. I was seeing powers and principalities firsthand.

I remember sitting on our bed, talking to that adversarial spirit inside of him, telling him that I would *not* allow him to destroy our family. I would not allow our son to go through the same pain that we had as children or permit these generational iniquities to take over. God and the Holy Spirit took over my mind. I began to lean completely on the word of God, believing fully in His promises, because He had already brought me through so much.

*I would not allow that adversarial spirit
inside of him to destroy our family.*

I couldn't seem to escape the parallel to my own parents—divorce, after my father had been pastoring for five years. I knew this was a relationship where God needed to come in fully.

I thought back to the night my brother-in-law died. My sister was screaming and crying at the hospital. My other sister told her she needed to cry out for Jesus. The presence of the Lord took over her body immediately, for when you mention the name of Jesus, demons flee. Saying the name of my Lord soothed my pain, and from this came a powerful song. I could call on no other name but Jesus at this point in my life.

JESUS

Music and Lyrics by Bonita McAfee Mitchell

First verse:

There is a name I love so dear.
It soothes my pain; it calms my fears.
That name is like no other name I know.
It comforts me everywhere I go.
The name is Jesus. There's comfort in that name.

Hook:

Jesus, oh how sweet the name.
You brought me through so many trials, Lord.
You carry me through the pouring rain.
Jesus, no other name I know
That can keep me from sinking too low.

Second verse:

The name I love, that name I fear;
In the midst of every one of my trials, Lord,
your name is oh so dear.
Even when I feel like I'm losing all control,
The Holy Spirit steps in and lets me know.
Call on the name Jesus
Because there's comfort in that name

Hook:

Jesus, oh how sweet the name.
You brought me through so many trials, Lord;
You carry me through the pouring rain.
Jesus, no other name I know
That can keep me from sinking too low.

Bridge:

I felt so out of control, Lord.
I thought I was gonna lose my mind.
I called on the name of Jesus;
He stepped in right on time.

I found myself thirsty and in the midst of a drought. I remembered the scripture that referred to a fountain: "For the Lamb at the center of the throne will be their shepherd; he will lead them to springs of living water. And God will wipe away every tear from their eyes" (Revelation 7:17). For those who do not yet know Him, that fountain is Jesus. Jesus extends himself over in abundance, like flowing water. He wants to know us, and so I started to seek Him more and more.

Jesus continued to turn my life around. The Holy Spirit started to lead me and instruct me on what to do to be a healthier, happier person. I listened, exercising and eating right, and I did become healthier and began losing weight. The word of God penetrated in the midst of so much pain, and that is when my life started to turn around. We need to always be reminded that God is in control. When we are in pain and need something to hold on to, He is there for us. He will never leave us comfortless.

God already knew all about me and my pain and sorrow. He knew all the secrets I knew and couldn't tell. I started to see and feel that Jesus would heal every broken place in a person's body and mind because that's where the enemy sets up house. It's his battlefield, but God tells us the battle has already been won—we just have to have unwavering faith and believe. In 2 Chronicles 20:15, it says, And he said, Hearken ye, all Judah, and ye inhabitants of Jerusalem, and thou king Jehoshaphat, Thus saith the Lord unto you. Be not afraid nor dismayed by reason of this great multitude; for the battle is not yours, but God's.

What many of us don't understand is that's just what the enemy does, pushing his way into your mind and heart to attempt to defeat your total being. He strategically tries his best to keep you out of the will of God. But Jesus wants us to live better than that, better than what I'd been living for over forty years.

It was a hard time, but if I kept my mind focused on Jesus, I could concentrate on thinking positive thoughts before I got out of bed in the morning. Our minds are like a playground for the devil. If he can keep us focused on the wrong thing around us or something we've done wrong, it keeps us from thinking about the one who can save us: Jesus.

> In your relationships with one another, have the same mindset as Christ Jesus: Who, being in very nature God, did not consider equality with God something to be used to His own advantage; rather, He made himself nothing by taking the very nature of a servant, being made in human likeness. And being found in appearance as a man, He humbled himself by becoming obedient to death— even death on a cross! Therefore God exalted Him to the highest place and gave Him the name that is above every name, that at the name of Jesus every knee should bow, in heaven and on earth and under the earth, and every tongue acknowledge that Jesus Christ is Lord, to the glory of God the Father.
>
> —Philippians 2:6-11

I had to cry out to Him every day, "Let this mind be in me which is in Christ Jesus." As I cried out to Jesus, he gave me this revelation in a song.

THIS MIND

Music and Lyrics by Bonita McAfee Mitchell

Let this mind be in me which is in Christ Jesus.
Let this mind be in me which is in Christ Jesus.
He's the author of my faith, the finisher of my soul.
Let this mind be in me which is in Christ Jesus.

The song goes on to say, "Let this love and peace be in me which is in Christ Jesus." The power is in the tongue, and I began to feel better the more I cried out to God.

I had to be strong and, in many ways and in matters of the spirit, run faster than my high school state track running times. I had to run fast to meet and try to find God. I was vulnerable like a baby and in pain, crying and scared all the time. That's why I needed to eat, sleep, and drink His Word so that He could talk to me and guide me through. I thought it might be difficult and even a little boring, but He introduced me to myself when I let Him in and allowed Him to have my mind and my heart.

In April 2010, I wrote and produced the first of two CDs under the Thread of Hope Records recording label. The first was a gospel CD titled *It Is Well with My Soul*; the second was a prevention/healing and liberating CD titled *Cherish Your Life,* which evolved from the song written after the young basketball player from my hometown committed suicide years earlier.

The first two CDs recorded on the Thread of Hope Recording label

After all my trials and tribulations, I'm confident and ready to spread the word of God through my book and my music. I want folks to know that if you die to self and allow the Holy Spirit to live in you, you can overcome anything. God is real, and all the storms I've experienced have only come upon me so that I can grow stronger and spread the message of victory through Jesus. I want to encourage other Christian married couples, broken little girls and boys, some much older now, and let them know they can make it. I am thoroughly convinced that God can fix anything for anyone who has a desire and the faith of a mustard seed. And Jesus said unto them, Because of your unbelief: for verily I say unto you, if ye have faith as a grain of mustard seed, ye shall say unto this mountain, Remove hence to yonder place; and it shall remove; and nothing shall be impossible unto you. (Matthew 17:20) .

Look up only to God and seek Him in the midst of your pain.

JUST SEEK HIS FACE

Music and Lyrics by Bonita McAfee Mitchell

First verse:

Let the peace of God, which surpasses all understanding,
it will guard your heart and mind through Christ Jesus.
In your intimate time of prayer, enter His presence and worship Him there,
just seek His face, He promised He would make away, He'll comfort you night
and day.

Hook:

Just seek God's face;
He promised He would make a way.
He'll comfort you every night and day.

Second verse:

Blessed are those who seek God with their whole heart,
not just His hand,
Not seeking everything my God can do for you,
Being steadfast and unmovable in His word,
Never doubting He'll take care of you.

Hook:

Just seek His face.
He promised He would make a way.
He'll comfort you every night and day.

Bridge:

Let this mind be in me
Which is in Christ Jesus.
I can be content, no matter what state I'm in.

I can do all things
through Christ who strengthens me.
I have faith in Him;
He supplies my every need.

Hook:

Just seek His face.
He promised He would make a way.
He'll comfort you every night and day.

Repeat verse 2:

Blessed are those who seek God with their whole heart,
not just His hand,
Not seeking everything my God can do for you,
Being steadfast and unmovable in His word,
Never doubting He'll take care of you.

Hook:

Just seek His face.
He promised He would make a way.
He'll comfort you every night and day.

Hook:

Just seek His face.
He promised He would make a way;
He'll comfort you every night and day.

After being separated for four years, I decided to file for divorce. But the Lord told me to stop. Kevin and I had been married twenty-three years, but we were still separated. I was dedicated to my ministry in California, while he continued to pastor in Michigan. Yet we were committed to continuing to work on our marriage, allowing Jesus and the Holy Spirit to heal us and bring us back together as a family.

9

MY JOURNEY TOWARD HEALING AND HOPE— AMAZING GRACE

I could have chosen to become very self-centered, sorrowful, depressed, and hopeless, giving up on life and everyone around me. Instead, I had to deny myself, pick up my cross, and follow Jesus to another level. My flesh had to die so His Holy Spirit could go to work inside me. I had to allow the power of Jesus to take complete control of my mind, heart, and soul, even if it meant suffering.

And he said to them all, "If any man will come after me, let him deny himself, and take up his cross daily, and follow me. For whosoever will save his life shall lose it: but whosoever will lose his life for my sake, the same shall save it."

—Luke 9:23–24

hen my husband, Kevin, told me he needed time away from me in August of 2008, my world could have come crashing down on me. But instead of falling apart, God saved me from despair by giving me a thirst for His word. The Holy Spirit directed me to read of the life of Jesus so that I might better understand what I was about to experience—the suffering, not for my sake, but for the sake of our

Father God. Romans 8:18 reads, "Consider that our present sufferings are not worth comparing with the glory that will be revealed in us." Suffering became a major part of my journey, allowing me to experience the love and power of Jesus like never before.

I couldn't make it without exercising daily for spiritual strength and mental/physical stress release. My mother's behavior and wisdom kicked in, and I began a real search for the Father who would never leave me.

Each morning, I read my Bible, finding stability for my mind and comfort for my soul in the familiar chapters and verses.

I also discovered that journaling positive thoughts, Bible verses, and encouraging words to myself could help set my mind and spirit right and give me inspired direction for the day. Some days that could be quite a challenge.

JOURNAL EXCERPT, MAY 2009

I woke up early this morning, closed in my right mind. My heart was feeling so heavy. When I laid down last night, things were not right. I woke up early this morning with the weight of the world in my heart. I couldn't explain it; my eyes were filled with tears. I didn't really know how to start to fix this situation I had fallen into.

The Holy Spirit spoke to me because worrying is sin. He put a song of hope on my mind. I got out of bed only to remember this: "I have told you these things, so that in me you may have peace. In this world you will have trouble. But take heart! I have overcome the world" (John 16:33). *Jesus had overcome this world and what I'm going through; I have to hold on to God's unchanging hands because there is nothing He cannot do.*

My real work was to believe truly that God sent Jesus to die and become my Lord and Savior. I couldn't just read the words any longer; I had to live and believe in the life of Jesus and walk in that obedience. I realized I wasn't doing it for me. I was doing it for others around me to see just how good God is in the middle of trying situations.

It was upon awakening that May morning that I questioned myself: *Is this really God (the Holy Spirit) speaking to me?*

I felt as if I were in a desolate land, an island on my own where I didn't know anybody but God. But in reality, the Holy Spirit had instructed me to visit the church that Sunday.

It had been oddly easy and comfortable being away from my husband after we'd separated. I couldn't see him or feel the pain of his spirit within the four walls of our home. However, going to church that Sunday, I felt a spirit of relief wash over me when Kevin, who was also my pastor, smiled at me and gave me a big hug during communion service. We truly loved each other but were under attack. His spirit was one of warmth and love, which he happily displayed before the congregation with his smile and obvious delight in seeing me. God knows it was His Holy Spirit humbling me because it was much bigger and more important than just I. God was not only growing me; He was growing everyone around me who witnessed and prayed for the movement of His hand to fix our marriage.

Kevin asked me to join the choir as they prepared to sing two selections during service. I asked a former choir member to lead a song, and she did, singing "Trouble in My Way." I followed her with "I Don't Believe He Brought Me This Far to Leave Me."

There was a sigh of relief from caring members, as well as Kevin and myself, thanking God for directing our every step. My heart was joyful, knowing that I'd married a man who truly loved God and cared so much about his commitment to staying in His will.

We all have experienced times in our lives where we've needed the Holy Spirit to lead, guide, and direct us in difficult times. It was such a blessing that my sister-in-law and niece visited the church that Sunday, always supporting with their loving spirits.

When I think back on that situation, it amazes me how two people can love each other so but become blindsided by the tricks of the mind and spirits. Neither Kevin nor I could see it coming. He was such a loving and caring pastor, always teaching the power of love and obedience. He thrived on making sure we all understood our personal role in having an intimate relationship with Jesus. It makes sense to me now how the adversary had plotted and planned a way he thought was going to destroy not only our family, but the church as well.

At the same time, I continued to pray, as did Kevin, wholeheartedly desiring to live righteously, fighting for our family and our one and only love—the one who never leaves us and is always there to comfort and speak to us: Jesus. He was then (and continues to be now) our guiding light, our way out of no way, our everything. He is the one we trust and count on to be here for us always.

When Kevin asked me to come back, returning home to Michigan was a big step of obedience for me. Life had been so unpredictable, and then, after I left, it had become peaceful and filled with all kinds of exciting possibilities, including landing a contract position in Los Angeles that paid five thousand dollars a month. I'd never dreamed that I would ever feel a sense of relief to be away from my best friend, my love for over forty-one years. The fact that I felt that relief was disturbing to me. Yet so much had happened in our relationship, and my husband had felt he needed time away from me to regroup.

Still, the parallels between my marriage and my parents' marriage bothered me. Like them, Kevin and I had been married for twenty years when we split up. Also, at the time of our separation, Kevin had been a pastor for five years, just like my father. What's more, like me at the time of my folks' divorce, our son was graduating high school and preparing to go off to college. It seemed unbelievable that I was reliving some of the worst pain I'd ever experienced in my life as my path unfolded in a way that so closely resembled that of my parents.

At a time when our son was getting ready to be off on his own, it was a time that should have been happy for my husband and me, and an opportunity to spend more time together, yet we were apart. It was a very painful time for our family.

I felt that as a pastor, Kevin should have had enough of God in his spirit to prevent this from happening. Even now, I can't explain the inner turmoil I felt about my husband. He had the ability to turn his God-filled spirit on or off, depending upon where he was. How could he transform his spirit into something completely different when he left the sanctuary and came home? I had never seen or experienced anything like it in my life. However, I started to realize the heart of man as well as demonic spirits that can take over one's spirit if it's not feeding and living on the word of God. The spirit is willing, but the flesh is weak and full of pride.

I woke up that Monday morning wondering what everyone was going to say about my returning home. Finally, the Holy Spirit drowned out those voices in my head by asking me, "When did the word *I* start to matter so much?"

It was then that I realized if only we could digest more of Jesus and His Holy Spirit, we would have more solid food upon which to feed and gain spiritual strength. If only we were better able to hear Him and be reminded of the suffering and humiliation He bore for us all, we'd be far less likely to worry about ourselves and what other people think of us.

I think of how different my family would have been had my father and mother been more aware of the tricks the adversary uses to set up and divide and conquer God's pastors and their families, all while destroying the churches at the same time. In our case, our family was never the same; the church my father pastored and for which my mother served as First Lady was split and has never recovered.

I know that Romans 8:28 says, "And we know that all things work together for good to those who love God, to those who are the called according to His purpose." You'd better believe it does, but there is suffering, even in the midst of "all things."

As the First Lady, I realize that I am in the midst of all things, a position where I'm a greater target for the enemy. As a result, I'm subject to more suffering and persecution. But my Bible tells me how I can profit from my trials. In James 1:2–6, the Word tells me, My brethren, count it all joy when ye fall into divers temptations; knowing this, that the trying of your faith worketh patience. But let patience have her perfect work, that you may be perfect and entire, wanting nothing. If any of you lack wisdom, let him ask of God, that giveth to all men liberally, and upbraideth not; and it shall be given him. But let him ask in faith, nothing wavering. For he that wavereth is like a wave of the sea driven with the wind and tossed.

Jesus suffered. He was humiliated—persecuted and crucified on the cross, with thorns on His head, nails in His hands and feet, and pierced in His side, His blood streaming down—just for us. All He asks of us is to remember His sacrifice. Forget about "I" and instead focus on "us," "we," and "they." He tells us in John 15:20, "Remember the word that I said unto you. The servant is not greater than his lord. If they have persecuted me, they will also persecute you; if they have kept my saying, they will keep yours also." Is the servant greater than His master? The answer is *no*.

I do not know anyone in this world who wants to experience pain. As for myself, I'm learning to hold on to humility and let go of pride. 1 Peter 5:5 tells us to be clothed with humility "for God resisteth the proud, and giveth grace to the humble." The Spirit instructed me a while ago to start studying the life of Jesus through daily reading in the New Testament, learning about Matthew, Luke, and John; reading about Abraham and Sarah and their faith; becoming more familiar with the faith of Job, as well as David and all he went through, yet God still called him a man after His own heart. It slowly started to make sense to me. However, I had a strong desire to seek God and be found.

Through it all, I continuously thought of the song "Amazing Grace": Amazing grace! How sweet the sound, That saved a wretch like me! I once was lost, but now am found; Was blind, but now I see.[1]

I started to sing and meditate on this song. For years, I'd heard it sung in church. Now it finally began to make sense to me.

It was only God's grace, His love and care, that carried me though this season and in fact still does. I'm finally learning to embrace the fact that *I don't matter*! I'm learning to die to my flesh every day so the Spirit of God can reign in my life. It is the only way for me to survive every day that I wake up and face the hindering spirits. It's only because Jesus lives. And the only thing that matters is the mission God has for me to do for His people and what I look like doing it. That's all that matters to God.

I'm also learning in this season of my life to bear others' crosses as well as my husband's cross. The Holy Spirit revealed to me that He wouldn't put more on me than I could abide and that now I must bear Kevin's cross as well. Of course, the Holy Spirit wouldn't tell me that if Kevin were beating or physically abusing me, but only to bear it if Kevin has a desire to live for God and be willing to die to the flesh to help save others—and thank God he did. The soul of my husband and the members at the church became more important to me than focusing on the infliction of pain I had to endure for Christ's sake.

Therefore, in the end, though I'm more of a target for the enemy as the First Lady, my position actually offers more opportunities for God to shine. My desire must always be for Jesus to be pleased with me as I allow His light to shine through me and as I allow myself to die to His will for others.

I've started to be very careful with my words and this tongue of mine,

---

[1] "Amazing Grace," John Newton (1725–1807), published in 1779.

not giving the adversary any power or ammunition. I won't even call out his name.

But to all of you ladies, as well as First Ladies out there, if we can stay in the race with Jesus, listening to the Holy Spirit and offering loving, godly support for our pastors (who also happen to be our husbands), the lives of millions of families in this world *will* change. We will no longer be faced with marriages dissolving and a staggering 80 percent of families being single-parent homes and an alarming rate of more than 30 percent of children in foster care.

God has given us His power and authority over the adversary when we find ourselves in situations that only He can handle. At that point, we must keep our eyes on Him and not be like Peter in Matthew 14:30: "But when he saw the wind boisterous, he was afraid; and beginning to sink, he cried, saying, Lord, save me." Jesus has never failed us, no matter how hard circumstances in the past and present tried to stop us. God was and still is always there. When we try to take matters into our own hands, He takes His hand off the situation. Our job is to give it to Him and leave it there with unwavering faith … He will come through.

10

MOVING INTO MY PURPOSE

My first two TV appearances … Dreams do come true … I sang the song "Amazing Grace" often, remembering all the times I'd heard my mother and others sing it. It opened my eyes to just how much grace God has and has always put into my life. For me, the line "I once was lost, but now am found; Was blind, but now I see, clarified the purpose of why I was created. It was so apparent that Jesus saved me to glorify Him. But I needed to experience the level of faith necessary to show others just how good He is. My purpose in life started to make sense to me. He was giving me wisdom for my journey and His power to endure the process.

But ye are a chosen generation, a royal priesthood, a holy nation, a peculiar people; that ye should show forth the praises of Him who hath called you out of darkness into His marvelous light.

—1 Peter 2:9

If my father and mother had never divorced, they would be going on over sixty years of marriage. Other couples have reached that milestone, and it's not as if they don't have issues. It's just that I think they decided somewhere along the journey that they would personally not allow the flesh to have victory over what God had joined together, what He had ordained for them before they were even born. Jeremiah 1:5 tells us, "Before I formed you in the womb, I knew you; before you were born, I sanctified you."

I knew I had to find my purpose outside of my husband's ministry and find what God had ordained for me before I was even born.

When you live your purpose, you will find, as I have, that God will present you with other areas of service upon which to focus. You'll discover that you get up in the morning differently; that you love and appreciate yourself and other church members the way God intended, acting lovingly and with kindness towards them, instead of feeling inferior to them because the adversary has told you lies.

So it was that God moved me into my purpose with Thread of Hope Records and the I'm Saving Myself Prevention/Intervention Program (ISM), *where* we utilize music and performing arts to address low self-esteem, bullying, cyberbullying, drugs, alcohol, violence, teen pregnancy, and suicide.

Because of all that had taken place in my life, I recognized that ISM reflected my own struggles. As a child and a teen with low self-esteem, I realized that many of my behaviors were dictated by my circumstances and feelings of low self-worth. I was brought up in an environment where there was little trust. I tried to move into relationships with my whole heart but found I just couldn't. Taking what I learned about myself and bringing it into the ISM program was what drove me to want to prevent those same things from happening in other young people's lives. If they could start when they were young to cast out those negative messages and identify that which keeps them stuck in the sins of past generations, they will be able to move forward into the future.

About three years ago—right around the time my husband and I first separated—I was overweight, both mentally and physically. I felt that because our son had graduated high school and was off to Full Sail University in Orlando, Florida, where he received a $42,000 Stevie Wonder scholarship, that Kevin really needed a break from me. But the Spirit would not allow me to go on thinking like that. Instead, I was instructed to start exercising and getting into shape to prepare for TV appearances to promote my singing career. I didn't question my instructions. I started to work out every day for one hour, five to six days a week. This allowed me to channel a lot of my stress and discouragement in more positive and healthy ways. I also changed my diet so that overeating wouldn't sabotage my efforts and cause me to gain more weight, which would have led to more misery and feelings of defeat. Of course, thinking about this inspired me to write a new song: "When I'm Feeling Defeated."

When I started to feel mentally defeated, I would begin to praise and worship God. I would sing various songs—"Thank you, Lord," "Jesus Loves Me," and "I Just Want to Praise You," to name a few—so that my spirit and mind would be filled with praise and welcome the Holy Spirit into my body and soul. By the time I was finished singing, the adversary had fled from my mind.

I've learned over the past four years that the adversary cannot handle praise. It must flee at the mention of the name of Jesus.

And just as I'd been told by the Holy Spirit, my career did indeed flourish. My first television appearance was on BET Network's Bobby Jones Gospel Celebrated 30 years with Al Mac Wil (a.k.a., Alice McAfee, Williams), my singing sister. My second TV appearance was on *Good Day LA*, which came about as a result of the Stevie Wonder House Full of Toys event, at which I was the choir teacher/director for his and Angela McAfee's nonprofit Musication program, in conjunction with my nonprofit ministry, I'm Saving Myself, and record label, Thread of Hope Records.

In the end, if we learn to listen to the Holy Spirit by clearing our minds, we will hear God speaking. He will manifest His word.

11

A PERSONAL RELATIONSHIP
WITH JESUS

Jesus was winning, and His Holy Spirit had taken complete control of my mind, heart, and soul. My purpose became quite simple: love and glorify my Father, who art in heaven. I had to allow my mind to stay on the word of God and live in every aspect of my life for others to see and desire the God I served so they could start to live in their purpose.

Jesus said unto him, "Thou shalt love the Lord thy God with all they heart, and with all they soul, and with all thy mind. This is the first and great commandment. And the second is like unto it, Thou shalt love thy neighbor as thyself. On these two commandments hang all the law and the prophets."

—Matthew 22:37–40

Even every one that is called by my name: for I have created him for my glory, I have formed him; yea, I have made him.

—Isaiah 43:7

was amazed when I actually started to embrace and take ownership of my purpose. In Matthew 17:20, the Bible says, "Truly, I tell you, if you have faith as small as a mustard seed, you can say to this mountain, 'Move from here to there,' and it will move. Nothing will be impossible for you."

I know that even with the smallest bit of faith and belief in God's promises, He will *never* let me down. It used to be easy for the adversary to plant doubt in my mind and keep me silently defeated. But as I read and studied God's Word, the Holy Spirit enabled me to replace those seeds of doubt with thanksgiving and praise for what God was already doing and what He was about to do in my life.

I would get up each morning filled with anticipation of His promises and what great things He had in store for me that day. I felt a sense of joy and victory when God would give me a sign or His Word would manifest, showing me I was listening and being obedient to His will.

I started to see and understand that when I moved as instructed by the Holy Spirit, God would move in my life. In James 2:14–17, God's Word reminds us, "What does it profit, my brethren, if someone says he has faith but does not have works? Can faith save him? If a brother or sister is naked and destitute of daily food, and one of you says to them, 'Depart in peace, be warmed and filled,' but you do not give them the things which are needed for the body, what does it profit? Thus, also faith by itself, if it does not have works, is dead." I had doubted myself and my ability to sing and speak for so long that I had never allowed the seed that God had planted in me before my birth to grow.

I started to read the book of Proverbs every day to obtain wisdom, knowledge, and understanding of God's Word. When I truly listened to the Word and understood it, then my eyes were opened and the shackles that bound me on the inside began to fall off.

I understand now what happens when I allow myself to submit to God and feel the pain while going through my storms. I give myself a visual picture of Jesus suffering, enduring the agony of crucifixion just for me, just for us. I'm learning to submit even when I can't fully understand, and I move out of God's way and accept His chastisement given with His loving hand to guide me along my way. I had to embrace what God allowed in my life and trust and have faith in Him to continue to guide me, even when I didn't know where I was going or what I was doing. I had to jump off the cliff and allow His Holy Spirit to catch me and direct me in the way He wanted me to go. I still can't believe everything I endured, always believing, with a doubt, that God would deliver me.

As I think back, I realize the Holy Spirit instructed me throughout my journey to do several things; I had no choice but to obey if I wanted a close relationship with Jesus. I had to act out of obedience and forgiveness. I spoke earlier of having to go back to Kevin for a time and move back into the house with him. Almost immediately, his spirit was uneasy, letting me know that he was unhappy, making me feel that I was invading his space. It could have only been God's blood and Holy Spirit that comforted me. I couldn't have done it on my own.

Kevin's and my relationship was taking hits we'd never experienced before. I remember that the last incident before I finally left for Los Angeles was so hurtful. We'd been at Bible study, and I'd left to go home to make dinner. Kevin told me he needed to make a run before coming home. After several hours, Kevin had still not arrived home and was not responding to my texts. I remember that finally, at 1 a.m., I texted him that I was going to file a missing person's report. He texted back that he was right where he needed to be. He stayed out about another hour and then returned home. That's when the Lord told me, "It's time to go."

As painful as this still sounds as I get to the end of this hurtful journey, if I hadn't listened to the Holy Spirit, I can't tell you where I would be right now. Maybe locked up in some mental hospital based on the level of trauma I was enduring and anger I was feeling. But God, Jesus, and His powerful comforting Holy Spirit took care of me.

In twenty-three years of marriage, Kevin and I had always respected each other enough never to do something like that to one another. But this time, he had crossed the line. This is how powerful principalities and powers are if we allow them a foothold in our families and daily lives. They will continue to live if we don't spiritually die and allow the Holy Spirit to take control.

God never stopped working with me, even when I went back to Los Angeles, where I continued working on the ISM program. Occasionally, I would travel back to Michigan to sing, speak, or work on The Salvation Army men's shelter ministry I'd started years earlier. God knows it would have been impossible to even think there was a Jesus and His Holy Spirit when I consider the level of embarrassment and pain I felt after seeing our family destroyed by the choices being made at that time. However, by being submissive to the Holy Spirit and not giving in to what I could see, God ultimately got the glory. He will always do so when we surrender all to Him, no matter the level and hurt, embarrassment, and pain. He will come to our rescue. Please know that He will come to yours as well. No matter how hard or bad your circumstances in your marriage or relationship, don't give up! God can fix it.

After I left, Kevin continually asked me to return to our home, but the Lord said, "No." It wasn't time yet.

Kevin wasn't focused enough on God or the area in which God needed him to grow, nor was I. He hadn't come to God or me in humility, for he didn't believe he'd done anything wrong. We both were struggling with a lot of pain.

For my part, I had to keep on walking righteously as best as I could with the Lord, asking Him for wisdom and guidance. All my alliance, my love, and yes, even my fear and unforgiveness, I had to give to the Lord. I felt that Kevin was continuing to be consumed with himself and his own needs and refused to seemingly live as righteously as God expected him to, I knew that I could not walk back into that relationship in which I would be living in Kevin's obedience, not God's. I needed to take the time to be where God needed me to be at that time. Please believe me that it was not easy, but it has proven to be rewarding over the years. God rewards us through our obedience to Him if we have the patience to wait on Him.

Journal Pages

Journal Pages

Journal Pages

Journal Pages

12

A MESSAGE TO FIRST LADIES AND SERVANTS OF GOD

I never wanted to be married to a preacher, let alone a pastor. God was showing me it was not my way but His way and I was to follow in the path so other First Ladies and servants would learn of my testimony and know they could make it through if they denied themselves. God had chosen Kevin, and I was a part of the package for the kingdom.

Ye have not chosen me, but I have chosen you, and ordained you, that ye should go and bring forth fruit, and that your fruit should remain: that whatsoever ye shall ask of the Father in my name, He may give it to you.

—John 15:16

s a little girl, I used to hear my mom sing so beautifully "He Knows How Much You Can Bear." I began to sing many songs that I remembered my mom singing, but that one in particular opened my eyes to the truth that God knew me. He knew how much I could bear, and I thanked Him continuously for being the architect of my life.

My sisters used to tell me of their personal encounters with the Holy Spirit. I'm now a living witness of what happens when we endure our storms with confidence and praise. It's such a blessing how the Lord shows up and shows out.

Inspired by the Spirit, I wrote the song "I Have Decided to Live for Jesus." In one part of the song I wrote, "I'm willing to bear the cross each day and stay in my Father's will. The times my spirit becomes vexed, He tells me to just stand still. To much that is given, much is required, no matter how hard the test; have faith and show love and I will do the rest." I'm trying to live these words every day. God knows it has been very challenging at times.

Yet the Holy Spirit required me to kill my flesh and take ownership of the fact that *I don't matter*; only what I do for Christ will last. When I talked to my husband, I felt major anxiety. But my spirit became at peace and I experienced clarity as I realized I was on the right track because Jesus was holding my hand. I allowed Him to guide my every step, and I felt His presence and anointing in my life. I felt calm happiness even as I traveled on a bumpy plane ride from New York to Philadelphia, then back to Los Angeles from the New York designer's shows.

I continue to have a sense of the Holy Spirit's peace and assurance that God is with me and that He will *never* leave me as long as I continue to seek His face.

First Ladies and servants of God, you can do this too. You can die to the flesh and allow God's spirit to reign! Pray and then watch God move. And remember to always love. Please trust His process for your life.

Servants of God, First Ladies, I applaud you for your undying strength, for your desire to die to flesh and allow God's love and spirit to reign and consume your total existence.

As difficult as it can be, remember always when Jesus was on the cross and He asked, "Father, Father, why hast thou forsaken me?" (Matthew 27:46). *That* was the beginning of life and freedom for us all. Jesus never said a mumbling word because He was focused and certain of the path God His Father had laid out for Him.

Jesus was ridiculed and humiliated, yet despite it all, He continued loving and staying on the path. He understood that His mission was not about Himself but about saving us from our sins.

Sometimes I like to throw myself a pity party, but God is not having it in this season of my life. He has given me enough of His spiritual nourishment through Kevin's strong wisdom, teaching, and preaching, as well as through the Spirit, that I'm eating hearty these days rather than desiring to remain on a newborn Christian's spiritual milk.

My life is *not* my own. My mind, body, and my entire being and existence belong to God my Father. He created you and me, and this entire world is His. He puts His stamp of approval on everything that happens to us. For example, consider Job 1:12, "The Lord said to Satan, 'Very well, then, everything he has is in your power, but on the man himself, do not lay a finger.' Then Satan went out from the presence of the Lord."

Our souls are the only things God will never approve the adversary taking and controlling. Everything else that God allows to happen in our lives—good or bad, as a result of our disobedience to His will—is an opportunity for our Father to shine through. To make this Christian journey, our faith and love for Jesus must be the dominating factor in our lives, living in the peace and presence of Jesus.

I have learned, First Ladies, to see God in everything that happens to me, and I praise and count it all joy.

> Consider it pure joy, my brothers and sisters, whenever
> you face trials of many kinds.
>
> —James 1:2.

Can it be very painful at times? Yes, but He tells us that we are more than conquerors ("No, in all these things we are more than conquerors through Him who loved us" [Romans 8:37]) and instructs us to put on the whole armor of God every morning before we even get out of bed ("Put on the full armor of God, so that you can take your stand against the devil's schemes" [Ephesians 6:11]).

I read Psalm 23 every morning to remind myself that no matter what's going on in my life, my Lord is my shepherd. I have allowed God to take His respective place in my life as my shepherd, and I shall not want for anything as long as He's leading my life.

I encourage you to start moving into the path to which God has called you and watch Him move after you do. "Moving" means your faith is not in yourself but in God to carry you, even when you don't completely understand it all. Moving requires that you love God enough to only be concerned about fearing and satisfying Him.

Everyone and everything else in my life fell into place when I surrendered my entire life to Jesus. I have an intimate personal relationship with Him now in which He talks to me throughout the day and directs me. It's only because of everything I've gone through that I've learned to lean only on Him, and as a result, He's come through for me every time.

I now see why it's so important for me to keep my heart and mind clear and to love like Jesus. Despite the fact that my profession is to look my best and to make my clients look beautiful, no matter what I wear or how I look, what really matters is that I am filled with the love of Christ inside. And that's what makes my outer beauty totally radiant. True beauty comes from the inside out.

It seems like only yesterday that I was that insecure child who felt like an ugly duckling. I didn't realize at the time that God was working on me to prepare me for such a time as now. He gave me the power at the age of ten to take control of how I felt about myself. I started to comb my own hair, putting ribbons in it, and shop for my own clothes. As a child, I made sure that my outer appearance was flawless, and that extended into my adulthood. I received recognition as "best dressed" my senior year of high school as well as in college. I thought I wanted to be a legal secretary in college and then discovered (after my grades dictated my true direction) that I couldn't escape my natural gifts of fashion and merchandising.

For years, my style prompted people to call me "First Lady," even before my husband became a preacher or pastor. My mother was such a great example of being beautiful from the inside out. As kids, we witnessed how she and my father treated people and offered their hearts in ways that gave of themselves to others. With this perspective, I finally figured out what God was trying to do with me. He needed me to understand that if I would take the power He had invested inside me and use it for His good, there would be nothing for which I could ever want. He took me through the circumstances of my life to understand that one day I would get old and my face, neck, legs, and arms would start to change, and there would be nothing I could do about it. And when He told me to leave my home for a time, He allowed me to think my husband had a younger lady and had gotten tired of me.

Therefore, I began doing a lot of soul-searching and crying out to God. I was a churchgoing sister every Sunday and became a First Lady at the age of forty (the same age as my mother). I started to realize that all my behavior was simply following traditions and that I had not really allowed God's Holy Spirit to take complete control of my life. I had it going on with my looks and clothing on the outside, but my insides were a complete mess. So I began to read the Word of God and got closer to Him. And then I felt my insides start to change and my confidence grow—not in myself or a man but in the man who would never leave me and would always be there for me, loving me despite how I felt about myself.

The Holy Spirit started to talk to me more because I was in a receptive place where I could hear and would listen. He would show me His hand in the smallest of things and places. I started to feel truly special, just like a little girl who had finally gotten the attention she'd always desired from her mom and dad. The confidence my daddy—my Heavenly Father—gave me was so real that my entire life changed from the inside out. I knew I was special because I had finally accepted the special power of God that was put inside of me before I was born. (Before I formed thee in the belly I knew thee; and before thou camest forth out of the womb I sanctified thee, and I ordained thee a prophet unto the nations. [Jeremiah 1:5].) Yes, before God formed me, He knew me in my mother's womb. He didn't make any mistakes when He created me. He made me beautiful and full of life so that I could give back to someone else what he had invested in me. Ecclesiastes 3:11 says, "He hath made everything beautiful in His time: also, He hath set the world in their heart, so that no man can find out the work that God maketh from the beginning to the end."

My life has changed for the best. God led me to change my hair color to blonde. He told me that my platform would help shed light on and tear down the "dumb blonde" syndrome. There is no such thing.

I notice people treating me differently now that I have blonde hair. I'd always wanted to see what it felt like being a blonde and had even tried it when I was younger, but the response now is overwhelming. I love the attention, but most of all, I'm proud to be more beautiful inside, where no one can really see. I love being kind to people when they look at me and don't expect me to be inviting. It seems that most people look at you and sum up who you are before you even open your mouth or before they've taken the time to get to know you.

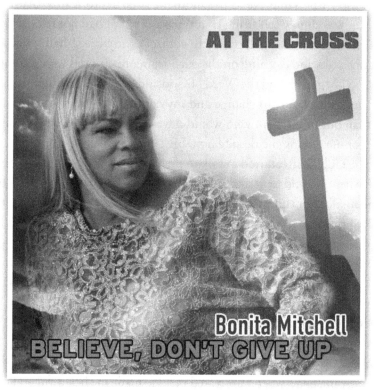

I'd always wanted to see what it felt like to be a blonde.

Ladies, what are they saying about you? Are you allowing your light to shine from the inside out? Or are you allowing the ills of your childhood to lead you down a path of insecurity, one on which you have the opportunity to affect people in a positive way, yet all they experience is your dark side because you refuse to submit to the loving power God invested in you before you were born?

We are experiencing an 80 percent rate of single-parent homes in this era. First Ladies, we can make a major difference in so many lives, but sometime fail to be on the front lines in love, helping these young ladies and young girls love themselves as God made them. Some of our lives and praise have become ineffective because of our position and the power we refuse to possess, as well as our refusing to die to flesh.

God has given me the opportunity to touch over twenty thousand young people through the ministry with Thread of Hope Records and I'm Saving Myself. This is a gift. God knew He could trust me to empower others faster than I would ever believe in myself. That's why God has allowed me to spend over fifteen years showing young girls and boys how important it is to utilize their gifts in a positive way in order to make healthy choices. Along the way, there were students who had given up on life but found hope after I was willing to offer them what God had entrusted me to give to them.

In the end, we know that kids—all kids, even the ones we ourselves were years and years ago—need someone looking out for them, helping them look out for themselves while trusting in God to show them the way. This is the beginning of our journey, during which it is most important to have a godly mentor for positive direction. I find that I'm more effective to others when I become more of the true woman of God He called me to be. When I began to discover my purpose and who it is that controls my being, life began to make more sense to me. It was never supposed to be about me. This life is one filled with opportunities to help others see the God in me and want to desire Him for themselves.

Be blessed!

FEED YOUR MIND WITH GOD'S WORD AND WATCH HIM CHANGE YOUR LIFE!

How do I start to understand your plans for me, Lord?

> "For I know the plans I have for you," declares the Lord, "plans to prosper you and not to harm you; plans to give you hope and a future."
>
> —Jeremiah 29:11

Lord, what plans do you have for me?

How do I put my belief in you, Jesus, into action?

> Jesus replied, "This is the work (service) that God asks of you: that you believe in the One Whom He has sent; that you cleave to, trust, rely on, and have faith in His Messenger."
>
> —John 6:29

The work of God …

What do I do when I'm trying to glorify you and I'm being talked about and persecuted to the point of doubting who you are?

> Everyone who is called by My name, and whom I have created for My glory, Whom I have formed, even whom I have made.
>
> —Isaiah 43:7

My purpose is to glorify God in everything I do.

Will I be liked because of the Jesus in me?

> And ye shall be hated of all men for my name's sake; but
> he that endureth to the end shall be saved.
>
> —Matthew 10:22

Prayer changes things! Believe!

Journal Pages

Journal Pages

Journal Pages

BONITA'S DAILY BIBLE PRESCRIPTION

To keep my eyes and my heart on the Lord requires that I spend part of each day, every day, meditating on His Word. I find that when I begin my day this way, I am filled with peace, direction, purpose, and inspiration. The Holy Spirit comes into my heart with joy, and I'm often moved to write both music and devotions after my daily meditation and prayer.

You too can discover a joyous and peaceful life when you follow my prescription and seek a relationship with Jesus every day. What follows are many of the Bible chapters and verses that touch my heart, along with devotions and songs I feel were divinely inspired during my time of hardship and pain.

Old Testament

Psalm 37 of David:

[1] Do not fret because of those who are evil
or be envious of those who do wrong;
[2] for like the grass they will soon wither,
like green plants they will soon die away.
[3] Trust in the LORD and do good;
dwell in the land and enjoy safe pasture.
[4] Take delight in the LORD,
and He will give you the desires of your heart.
[5] Commit your way to the LORD;
trust in Him and He will do this:
[6] He will make your righteous reward shine like the dawn,
your vindication like the noonday sun.
[7] Be still before the LORD
and wait patiently for Him;
do not fret when people succeed in their ways,
when they carry out their wicked schemes.
[8] Refrain from anger and turn from wrath;

do not fret—it leads only to evil.
[9] For those who are evil will be destroyed,
but those who hope in the LORD will inherit the land.
[10] A little while, and the wicked will be no more;
though you look for them, they will not be found.
[11] But the meek will inherit the land
and enjoy peace and prosperity.
[12] The wicked plot against the righteous
and gnash their teeth at them;
[13] but the Lord laughs at the wicked,
for He knows their day is coming.
[14] The wicked draw the sword
and bend the bow
to bring down the poor and needy,
to slay those whose ways are upright.
[15] But their swords will pierce their own hearts,
and their bows will be broken.
[16] Better the little that the righteous have
than the wealth of many wicked;
[17] for the power of the wicked will be broken,
but the LORD upholds the righteous.
[18] The blameless spend their days under the LORD's care,
and their inheritance will endure forever.
[19] In times of disaster they will not wither;
in days of famine they will enjoy plenty.
[20] But the wicked will perish:
Though the LORD's enemies are like the flowers of the field,
they will be consumed, they will go up in smoke.
[21] The wicked borrow and do not repay,
but the righteous give generously;
[22] those the LORD blesses will inherit the land,
but those He curses will be destroyed.
[23] The LORD makes firm the steps
of the one who delights in Him;
[24] though he may stumble, he will not fall,
for the LORD upholds him with His hand.

²⁵ I was young and now I am old,
yet I have never seen the righteous forsaken
or their children begging bread.
²⁶ They are always generous and lend freely;
their children will be a blessing.
²⁷ Turn from evil and do good;
then you will dwell in the land forever.
²⁸ For the LORD loves the just
and will not forsake His faithful ones.
Wrongdoers will be completely destroyed;
the offspring of the wicked will perish.
²⁹ The righteous will inherit the land
and dwell in it forever.
³⁰ The mouths of the righteous utter wisdom,
and their tongues speak what is just.
³¹ The law of their God is in their hearts;
their feet do not slip.
³² The wicked lie in wait for the righteous,
intent on putting them to death;
³³ but the LORD will not leave them in the power of the wicked
or let them be condemned when brought to trial.
³⁴ Hope in the LORD
and keep His way.
He will exalt you to inherit the land;
when the wicked are destroyed, you will see it.
³⁵ I have seen a wicked and ruthless man
flourishing like a luxuriant native tree,
³⁶ but he soon passed away and was no more;
though I looked for him, he could not be found.
³⁷ Consider the blameless, observe the upright;
a future awaits those who seek peace.
³⁸ But all sinners will be destroyed;
there will be no future for the wicked.
³⁹ The salvation of the righteous comes from the LORD;
He is their stronghold in time of trouble.
⁴⁰ The LORD helps them and delivers them;

He delivers them from the wicked and saves them,
because they take refuge in Him.

Psalm 91:

[1] Whoever dwells in the shelter of the Most High
will rest in the shadow of the Almighty.
[2] I will say of the Lord, "He is my refuge and my fortress,
my God, in whom I trust."
[3] Surely He will save you
from the fowler's snare
and from the deadly pestilence.
[4] He will cover you with His feathers,
and under His wings you will find refuge;
His faithfulness will be your shield and rampart.
[5] You will not fear the terror of night,
nor the arrow that flies by day,
[6] nor the pestilence that stalks in the darkness,
nor the plague that destroys at midday.
[7] A thousand may fall at your side,
ten thousand at your right hand,
but it will not come near you.
[8] You will only observe with your eyes
and see the punishment of the wicked.
[9] If you say, "The Lord is my refuge,"
and you make the Most High your dwelling,
[10] no harm will overtake you,
no disaster will come near your tent.
[11] For He will command His angels concerning you
to guard you in all your ways;
[12] they will lift you up in their hands,
so that you will not strike your foot against a stone.
[13] You will tread on the lion and the cobra;
you will trample the great lion and the serpent.
[14] "Because he loves me," says the Lord, "I will rescue him;
I will protect him, for he acknowledges my name.

¹⁵ He will call on me, and I will answer him;
I will be with him in trouble,
I will deliver him and honor him.
¹⁶ With long life I will satisfy him
and show him my salvation."

Psalm 34:

I will bless the LORD at all times;
His praise shall continually be in my mouth.
² My soul makes its boast in the LORD;
let the humble hear and be glad.
³ Oh, magnify the LORD with me,
and let us exalt His name together!
⁴ I sought the LORD, and He answered me
and delivered me from all my fears.
⁵ Those who look to Him are radiant,
and their faces shall never be ashamed.
⁶ This poor man cried, and the LORD heard him
and saved him out of all his troubles.
⁷ The angel of the LORD encamps
around those who fear Him, and delivers them.
⁸ Oh, taste and see that the LORD is good!
Blessed is the man who takes refuge in Him!
⁹ Oh, fear the LORD, you His saints,
for those who fear Him have no lack!
¹⁰ The young lions suffer want and hunger;
but those who seek the LORD lack no good thing.
¹¹ Come, O children, listen to me;
I will teach you the fear of the LORD.
¹² What man is there who desires life
and loves many days, that he may see good?
¹³ Keep your tongue from evil
and your lips from speaking deceit.
¹⁴ Turn away from evil and do good;
seek peace and pursue it.

[15] The eyes of the LORD are toward the righteous
and His ears toward their cry.
[16] The face of the LORD is against those who do evil,
to cut off the memory of them from the earth.
[17] When the righteous cry for help, the LORD hears
and delivers them out of all their troubles.
[18] The LORD is near to the brokenhearted
and saves the crushed in spirit.
[19] Many are the afflictions of the righteous,
but the LORD delivers him out of them all.
[20] He keeps all his bones;
not one of them is broken.
[21] Affliction will slay the wicked,
and those who hate the righteous will be condemned.
[22] The LORD redeems the life of His servants;
none of those who take refuge in Him will be condemned.

Psalm 23:

The LORD is my shepherd, I lack nothing.
[2] He makes me lie down in green pastures,
He leads me beside quiet waters,
[3] He refreshes my soul.
He guides me along the right paths
for His name's sake.
[4] Even though I walk
through the darkest valley,
I will fear no evil,
for you are with me;
Your rod and your staff,
they comfort me.
[5] You prepare a table before me
in the presence of my enemies.
You anoint my head with oil;
my cup overflows.
[6] Surely your goodness and love will follow me

all the days of my life,
and I will dwell in the house of the LORD
forever.

Proverbs:

Read one chapter per day, beginning with chapter 1.

Psalms:

Read three books per day, beginning with chapter 1.

New Testament

Read three verses per day, beginning with chapter 1.

Devotions

When I'm feeling defeated, the Holy Spirit reminds me to call on Jesus's name. When I'm feeling defeated, the Word tells me every day God that is the same because every time He's brought me out. I know there is nothing God can't do. Therefore, when I'm feeling defeated, I start to worship and praise my way through it. John 16:33 tells me, "I have overcome the world." Revelations 17:14 tells me, These shall make war with the Lamb, and the Lamb shall overcome them: for he is Lord of lords, and King of kings: I know God can handle it without a doubt. So when I'm feeling defeated, I start to praise and worship my way out. Thank you, Lord.

People are hurting, wondering what I did wrong. Relationships are failing as if God has fallen from His throne. Children are in excruciating pain, covering it with multiple substances, trying to avoid the rain.

We need a word from you, Lord. We need to seek you and know nothing in our lives can manifest without you. You're the only way to go. There's no way to get around the storm. We all will experience tribulations in this world. But with you, Lord, we have the victory. We do not have to walk around in defeat continually. We do have the victory.

As much as we read and learn about you, all the many times you have always come through, why can't I remember that this can be my test? The weight gets so very hard, multiplying pressure in my chest. We do know we are more than conquerors in Jesus Christ. Just have to continue to tell the devil he's a liar.

We will make it through all these principalities. Understanding that you, God, are all we need. No matter how difficult or hard things may be, our faith and trust will always be in Thee. Thank you, Lord.

~

Dear Lord, I know this is all a part of a season in my life. I'm standing on your promises and your will to do right. It does not matter what I'm going through. It's not about me but all about you. I'm experiencing persecution daily. Lord I'm seeking your word, wisdom, knowledge, and understanding along the way. Opening my eyes and heart to continue to see the power and love you've invested in me. By sending your only son, Jesus, for all of my sins, who died and conquered death for me, not to ever give in or give up on you, no matter what I'm going through. Is the servant greater than his master?

> Remember the word that I said unto you, the servant is not greater than his lord. If they have persecuted me, they will also persecute you; if they have kept my saying, they will keep yours also
>
> —John 15:20

No, so suffering for Christ's namesake ...

> For even hereunto were ye called: because Christ also suffered for us, leaving us an example, that ye should follow His steps.
>
> —1 Peter 2:2

I'm waiting on You Jesus, knowing long-suffering produces patience and love that can only come from you, dear Lord above. All heavens and earth was created for You. It's all worth it. Keep me strong in your care as I walk this path in thin air. Your loving hand guiding me all the way. Helping me see my dark path by telling me to stand still and see the

Salvation of the Lord. I love you; I love you. I worship and adore you, Lord. Can't make it without you, Lord. Please keep me in your care. Thank you, Lord!

～

We have all heard the slogan "A mind is a terrible thing to waste." I think about that a little differently these days. I focus on the waste—the garbage—and the fact that the mind is the storage place where I put disposable items and how they can kill me as I go through my day-to-day life. I am what I think and whatever I deposit into my mind and body.

The Bible says in Philippians 2:5, "Let this mind be in me which is in Christ Jesus." I began to really focus my mind on this passage of scripture and meditate on it to the point of not only writing one song but two—"God Will Give You Peace if You Keep Your Mind Stayed on Thee," followed by "Let This Mind."

I pleaded with God to take control of my mind and give me peace in the midst of my storms (which seemed to be more like major earthquakes). He answered my prayers and at the same time showed me how I must replace the negative thoughts clouding and taking control of my mind with positive thoughts such as, *How would Jesus handle this?* and *What would Jesus do?*

It all went back to making certain the adversary did not have the ability to build his home in any open space in my mind. I stopped giving him the power to have free rein of my mind and senses. He had to flee every time I mentioned or thought of the name of Jesus.

God gives us choices so we can show Him just how much faith and trust we have in living for Him and listening to His Word, all while being a doer of His word. He also gives us choices so we can understand that by the power He invested in us, we can control our thinking and every bit of our existence.

I am learning to use the thought process of Jesus continuously so that my days and nights are not affected by the adversary's attempts to reign in my life—and especially in my mind. I try to remember God's Word and scriptures strategically, along with positive godly songs to fill every space of my brain so that I can stay in the presence of the Lord. I can truly say that things do not affect me as they used to now that I'm keeping my mind on Jesus and seeing and finding Him in every situation and everything that happens to me in my life. I understand now that everything has to go through Him before it gets to me. God knows exactly what I can handle. He allows me to weather the storms so that I might build my faith and trust in Him and demonstrate to others just how effective He can be in our lives when we allow Him to reign instead of our pride. Remember, we don't matter—only what we can do for Christ does.

SONGS

MY SONGS OF INSPIRATION AND COMFORT

HE DID IT JUST FOR ME

Music and Lyrics by Bonita McAfee Mitchell
Copyright © 2012 by All Heart Publishing

Hook:

He did it just for me, sacrificed His life on Calvary,
To chase my sins away, and now I'm happy to say
Jesus is the way,
Jesus is the way.

Ad-lib:

The way to truth, love, and life,
Jesus is the way

Lead singer:

Jesus did it just for me.
He saved my soul; now I can see
He's the light of my day.
He moves every dark cloud out of my way.
Jesus is the way,
The way to truth, love, and life.
Jesus is the way.

Lead singer:

Jesus did it just for me;
His word gives me victory.
I'm happy now to say
Jesus Christ is the only way.
Jesus is the way,
The way to truth, love, and life.
Jesus is the way.

Bridge:

He brightens every dark cloud in my heart,
And my life belongs to Him.
He gives me strength when I'm weak;
I owe it all to thee.
Jesus is the way.

Ad-lib:

Try Him; get to know Him.
Jesus is the way.
Doesn't matter what you're going through.
Jesus is the way.
He changed my life, cleaned me from all the misery and strife.
Jesus is the way.
He turned my night into day;
Jesus is the only way.

IF YOU BELIEVE*

Music and Lyrics by Bonita McAfee Mitchell
Copyright © 2012 by All Heart Publishing

First Verse:

If you believe, you will achieve.
Having faith and trust in God, you will succeed.
If you believe, try living your dreams,
No matter what your circumstances may be.
Don't give up; you have come too far to turn around.
Keep looking up; God is taking you to higher ground.
Believe and surrender all to Thee.

Chorus:

Don't give up.
Keep looking up

Second Verse:

If you believe, you will succeed,
No matter what your circumstances may be.
If you believe in what you cannot see,
God will reward this kind of faith.
It is the key.
Don't give up; you have come too far to turn around.
Keep looking up; God is leading you to higher ground.
Believe and surrender all to Thee.

Chorus:

Don't give up.
Keep looking up

Bridge:

I know it's hard for you to understand.
God knows, so put it in the Master's hand
And give it all to Thee
Thank you, Lord!

*Inspired by friends to write this, I rearranged this composition for my niece's wedding. It is great song for Christian marriages.

To listen to this song, please go to bonitamitchell.com

LET THIS MIND

Music and Lyrics by Bonita McAfee Mitchell

I knew I had to take back control of my mind. I had to turn the phone off—and all the unhealthy noise and conversations—or push the mute button so I could hear the Holy Spirit talking to me, that small voice speaking and giving me my directions for the day and for this season. I wrote a song to remind me to keep my mind on Christ:

Let this mind be in me which is in Christ Jesus.
Let this mind be in me which is in Christ Jesus.
He's the author of my faith,
The finisher of my soul.
Let this mind be in me which is in Christ Jesus.
Let this peace be in me which is in Christ Jesus.
Let this peace be in me which is in Christ Jesus.
He's the author of my faith,
The finisher of my soul.
Let this peace be in me which is in Christ Jesus.
Let this love be in me which is in Christ Jesus.
Let this love be in me which is in Christ Jesus.
He's the author of my faith,
The finisher of my soul.
Let this love be in me which is in Christ Jesus

WHEN I'M FEELING DEFEATED

Music and Lyrics by Bonita McAfee Mitchell

Hook:

When I'm feeling defeated, The Holy Spirit reminds me to call on Jesus's name.
When I'm feeling defeated, Every day He is the same.
'Cause all the times He's brought me out, I know God can handle it without a doubt
When I'm feeling defeated, I start to praise and worship my way out.

First verse:

It gets hard sometimes staying on the Lord's side.
Burdens press you down—no friends to be found.
There's one I call on; His name is Jesus, God's son.
He fills my soul with love and assures me this race He's won

Hook:

When I'm feeling defeated,
The Holy Spirit reminds me to call on Jesus's name.
When I'm feeling defeated,
Every day He is the same
Cause all the times He's brought me out
I know God can handle it without a doubt
When I'm feeling defeated,
I start to praise and worship my way out.

Second verse:

There's nothing in this world my God cannot handle,
Even those times I cry with all the pain inside.
He comforts me and lets me know

He will never, ever leave me or let me go.
Just hold to His unchanging hand;
He will lead you to the promise land.

Hook:

When I'm feeling defeated,
The Holy Spirit reminds me to call on Jesus's name.
When I'm feeling defeated,
Every day He is the same
'Cause all the times He's brought me out
I know God can handle it without a doubt
When I'm feeling defeated,
I start to praise and worship my way out.

Bridge:

"I have overcome the world;
The Lamb has overcome defeat
Because He's the Lord of lords
And King of kings,
I am an heir of the King."

GOD IS BUILDING ME FROM THE INSIDE OUT

Music and Lyrics by Bonita McAfee Mitchell

Hook:

God is building me every day
From the inside out,
For He knows everything about me
From the very start.
God wants to heal all of my pride
So His Holy Spirit can abide.
God is building me every day
From the inside out.

THREAD OF HOPE RECORDS'
SOLUTIONS THROUGH
WORDS AND MUSIC

tohrecords.com

Our History

Thread of Hope Records (TOHR) focuses on our abstinence nonprofit, I'm Saving Myself, while running in-school and after-school programming, utilizing it's very own Healthy Body, Healthy Mind curriculum. Students can find their voice, gifts, and talent in a safe and happy environment led by parents and student leaders.

The purpose behind the music is to build a foundation through music and the arts that will tackle and raise the consciousness on subject matters that are plaguing today's youth.

Customers who purchase our journals and music from Thread of Hope Records will do so because of not only the appealing content and sound of each journal and composition but also because each journal and recording deals so eloquently and directly with problems and situations that the reader and listener may find difficult to address.

Thread of Hope Records will strive to fill the void created by so many of the issues faced by today's youth (low self-esteem, bullying, cyberbullying, suicide, drugs, alcohol, teen pregnancy, and so forth) by giving hope and offering healing through words, music, and the arts.

The mission of Thread of Hope Records is to work with youth and families who are struggling. Through journaling and therapeutic music, multimedia, and art, we will try to identify areas of pain and shine a light into what can sometimes be a dark space in a child's world. By offering this hope and light through these vehicles, we believe we can help these young people and families see their dreams become reality.

We have produced various journals for kids and families from pre-K through grade two, called "I Am Special." For kids from third grade through college age, we offer journals called "Just Me" to build self-esteem; "Cherish Your Life" to build confidence and awareness of depression, trauma, and suicide; "These Feeling's I've Got," which helps identify healthy and unhealthy feelings that can lead to success or negative choices; and "Dreams," which inspires hope and cherished aspirations.

I'm Saving Myself

imsavingmyself.org

Prevention and Intervention Program

Using music and performing arts to help youth make healthy choices for lifelong success

I'm Saving Myself (ISM) was birthed in 2001, after the tragic suicide of a popular high school student. At that time, Bonita McAfee Mitchell (who is now the executive director of ISM and CEO of Thread of Hope Records) was asked by an Eau Claire, Michigan, high school counselor if she would be willing to help the students move through their grieving process.

They asked that Bonita present the interactive musical performance she'd produced and had been performing in Los Angeles and Sacramento, California, for nearly four years. The production introduced a genre of music that highlighted social issues that impact young people yet are not readily discussed by youth.

In the production, young performers advocate for healthy lifestyle choices for their peers. It was during one of these school productions, titled "Celebrate Life and Pursue Your Dreams," that Bonita was made aware of two other young people who were planning to commit suicide. One was a youth working within the production; the other was a youth who attended the performance. One particular song in that performance served to deter these young people from following through with their suicide plans. It addressed teen pregnancy prevention and was titled "I'm Saving Myself." Of course, that composition became the organization's theme song. I'm Saving Myself (ISM) partnered with various churches to produced its Purity Ceremony, where over 100 youth committed to abstinence until marriage.

Just Me Journal

Cherish Your Life Journal

These Feelings I've Got Journal

Dreams Journal

We have produced our "I Am Special" book with a CD, journal, and coloring books for parents and students ages pre-K through second grade. These help students who are having challenges with reading, along with building self-esteem.

I Am Special Book

Finally, at Thread of Hope Records, we want to raise our communities' consciousness regarding trauma, as well as teen and parent issues, while helping to identify and address problems and areas of pain before tragedies occur.

THE PURPOSE BEHIND
MY LIFE'S JOURNEY

This book was written to allow you and me to see my life's journey of the unseen. It serves as my road map of faith when I'm faced with various opportunities for Jesus to reign in my life. It quickly reminds me that if He brought me through then, He certainly *will* bring me through now.

Another reason I had to document these various opportunities in my life was because I learned that when things were out of control, I had to just say, "I trust you, Jesus" and live that truth. Whatever is prohibiting you from moving forward, submit and just trust God.

His precious Holy Spirit that lives in you and me answered my call and *will* answer yours as well. Get in your quiet place and exercise your God-given faith. I couldn't see or understand what was happening to me, but I had living faith. Because it was so small while I was growing up, I didn't even realize I had it. Now I know that scripture grows enormously as we keep watering it, reading God's Word, His Holy Bible, and living it, in spite of challenges, which are actually opportunities I faced every day. I had to continue walk the life of trusting God in my daily life.

I realize now that my life has never been about me as much as it is allowing people to see and experience my glorifying Jesus so they can start to trust the Him in me. I'm free now. My mind is filled with so much of His Word that even during the dark seconds, and minutes, or hours of rain and clouds, His work becomes my living water to brighten my inner world into the garden of His heart and love for me. I start to whisper, "I trust you, Jesus" when I'm full of so much pain. He meets me as soon as I reach out to Him by reminding me, "For His anger endureth but a moment; in His favor is life; weeping may endure for a night, but joy cometh in the morning" (Psalm 30:5). "No weapon that is formed against thee shall prosper; and every tongue that shall rise against thee in judgment thou shalt condemn. This is the heritage of the servants of the Lord, and their righteousness is of me, saith the Lord" (Isaiah 54:17).

I invite you to a life of opportunity and freedom by believing and remembering that God did send His son. Our real work every day is to believe in Him and start to understand that every day our lives are about glorifying Jesus. We must allow others to see Him in us so that they too want and desire to know Him by the love—which is not ours but His—we are willing to share.

Enjoy your mental journey with me as I have outlined the details of my life that have shaped me to be the loving woman of God I am today. Join me in my quest with God the Father, God the Son, and God the Holy Spirit. Witness how they are one and worked in different aspects of my life, knowing that they can work in yours as well.

As we come to the end of my journey in *The First Lady The Process To My Purpose Believe, Don't Give Up!* thank you for desiring to have faith and trust in our Creator of heaven and Earth; our Creator knows us all and will never put more on us than we can bear. "There hath no temptation taken you but such as is common to man: but God is faithful, who will not suffer you to be tempted above that ye are able; but will with the temptation also make a way to escape, that ye may be able to bear it" (1 Corinthians 10:13). Jesus knows us better than we know ourselves. We just have to have unwavering faith and allow His Holy Spirit to lead, guide, and direct our every step.

Printed in the United States
by Baker & Taylor Publisher Services